The Gypsy Debate

Can Discourse Control?

Joanna Richardson

imprint-academic.com

Published in the UK by
Imprint Academic, PO Box 200, Exeter EX5 5YX, UK

Published in the USA by
Imprint Academic, Philosophy Documentation Center
PO Box 7147, Charlottesville, VA 22906-7147, USA

ISBN-10 1 84540 057 7
ISBN-13 9781845400576

A CIP catalogue record for this book is available from the
British Library and US Library of Congress

Contents

Chapter One

Introduction

They are scum, and I use the word advisedly. People who do
what these people have done do not deserve the same human
rights as my decent constituents going about their everyday
lives. (MacKay, 2002)

Andrew MacKay, MP for Bracknell, stated his opinion (above) as
part of a House of Commons debate on an unauthorised encampment of Gypsies and Travellers. Whilst this is an extreme view, it is
not an isolated one. This type of sentiment is echoed in other political
and public discourse around Gypsies and Travellers. Such discourse
reflects antipathy towards Gypsies and Travellers; but it also has a
power to control and shape the treatment of this minority group, by
the rest of society.

The debate surrounding Gypsies and Travellers is current in
Whitehall, town halls and in the media. In the media, issues of site
provision and discrimination are examined in newspapers such as
the Guardian (Bowers and Benjamin, 2004 and Barkham, 2004).
These examples of coverage of the issues are largely positive, as is
the news (Beunderman, 2004) that the first Roma MEP was elected to
the European parliament. Despite positive moves to debate the
issues, there is also an increase in negative discursive debate (Greenhill, 2004, Kelly, 2004, Levy, 2004 and Long, 2004). Largely, this negative coverage is centred upon the issue of the cost of dealing with
planning appeals and unauthorised sites. There is also recognition
that Gypsies and Travellers are subject to negative, discriminatory
discourse that would not be acceptable against other Black and
Minority Ethnic communities (Asthana, 2004).

The hypothesis of the book is that discourse can be used as a tool to
control those who refuse to conform to societal norms (for instance
living in a permanent dwelling), and it looks specifically at Gypsies
and Travellers as a controlled group. Discourse can be controlling
(Foucault, 1977, 1999 and 2003) but it is perhaps more the actions that

discriminatory discourse can lead to that are the real mechanisms of control.

> People don't like travellers … The operation wasn't just about arresting people, but also part of a 'decommissioning exercise', hitting people so hard and ruining their homes so they'll think twice about leading this lifestyle. (Lodge, 2004: 73)

This is an extreme example of the suggestion or coercion of Gypsies and Travellers to lead a settled life. Lodge and his fellow Travellers were arrested and allegedly hit by the police, when they were evicted from an unauthorised encampment. It was perceived by the Travellers that they were being punished for their lifestyle choice. The example demonstrates the physical manifestation of discriminatory discourse surrounding Gypsies and Travellers, and it outlines the experience of one Traveller's treatment by the police. It is not the only example. A report in the Observer (McLaughlin, 2005) discussed the issues around a programme of forced sterilisation for Gypsy women in the Czech Republic. This is not a historical account of previous problems, it is a report on what is happening now, to a minority group, in Europe. If discriminatory discourse is seen as acceptable (for instance in the House of Commons, MacKay, 2002) and this then manifests itself in controlling action—either by the police, or by members of the public, or even by members of the Czech health service—there is a place for examination of the notion of discourse as control.

Through a variety of methodological approaches (see Fig. 1), a number of themes were found which support the notion that discourse can be used to heighten the 'otherness' of Gypsies and Travellers. This has the effect of placing them under the surveillant gaze of society, and it is a form of control. It is the interpretation of discourse which can result in discriminatory policies and legislation. For instance, my research found that 'mess' and 'cost' was a core theme in public discourse and this is reflected in the wording of legislation and local policy. The responsibilities of Gypsies, to keep sites tidy, outweigh their rights to accommodation. There appeared to be a discursive link between anti-social behaviour and Gypsies and Travellers and, again, this is demonstrated in the law (Anti-Social Behaviour Act, 2003, Part Seven).

Approach	Methodology
Media Analysis	Search of English and Welsh national and local newspapers for the month of October 2003, using Lexis Nexis database. 54 articles were found, eight were discounted (e.g they referred to a football team called the Gypsies), 13 articles were viewed as being largely positive, with the remaining 33 articles having a negative focus. Coding and analysis of the articles was conducted using NVIVO software.
Planning Consultation in a Local Authority	This was the only local authority debating new site provision at the time (December 2003). The public meeting allowed for the researcher to be observer, without any direct involvement in the discussion. Ongoing communication with the Planning Officer also facilitated access to previous consultation information where 598 responses from the public had been received by the council.
Gypsy/Traveller Focus Groups	A series of four focus groups was held, with a mixture of Romany Gypsies and Irish Travellers, from November to early December 2003.

Figure 1: Summary of Methodological Approach

By highlighting some of the reasons behind the current discriminatory discourse around Gypsies and Travellers, it is hoped that the debate can move on from looking at the practical problems faced (the symptoms) to examine the causes of these issues. If the motive behind the discourse is discussed, a solution could be considered. This book focuses on uncovering the theories behind the Gypsy/Traveller discourse.

Emerging Themes

From the analysis of the primary research, I noted some emerging key themes in the discourse around Gypsies and Travellers.

Emerging Key Themes

- Cost and mess
- Labelling — Gypsies or Travellers?
- Folk devils   *Crime?*
- Influx and invasion

In addition to these discursive themes was an analytical theme, namely:

- Who is talking about Gypsies and Travellers?

Figure 2: Emerging Key Themes

Some of these themes are reflected in the relevant literature, particularly issues surrounding 'cost and mess' and labelling. One theme which was apparent in my review of the literature was crime (for instance Leudar and Nekvapil, 2000); however this was not reflected in my own research. The issue of cost and mess seemed to be far higher up the agenda.

These themes are discussed throughout the book. They are used as examples and explanations of controlling discourse, within a theoretical framework (outlined in chapter three) and are discussed in detail in chapters six and seven.

Definitions

It is important to examine some of the terms that are used in the book. 'Gypsies and Travellers' is used throughout, as a term to discuss Romany Gypsies, Irish Travellers and New Travellers, as a whole group. If a specific group of Gypsies and Travellers is referred to then they will be identified separately; otherwise Gypsies and Travellers are discussed together. The terms are also used with capital letters to denote their recognition as a Black and Minority Ethnic Group. This recognition, is highlighted by Gypsies and Travellers themselves, and by the Commission for Racial Equality; it has legal definition under the Race Relations Act 1976, for Gypsies following the case of *CRE V Dutton* (1989) 1 All ER 306; and for Irish Travellers in the case of *O'Leary and others v Punch Retail and others* (2000). A definition of a 'Gypsy' or 'Traveller' is not simple; however a commonly used legal definition is from the Caravan Sites and Control of Development Act 1960 s24 (as amended by the Criminal Justice and Public Order Act 1994 s80) which states that Gypsies and Travellers are *'persons of nomadic habit of life, whatever their race or origin'*.

The legal definition refers to nomadism as the defining characteristic of a Gypsy or Traveller. However, this is difficult because not all Gypsies and Travellers are nomadic, some have moved into permanent housing because there has been no alternative. There is also the issue of ethnicity; the Commission for Racial Equality (CRE) makes clear that Romany Gypsies and Irish Travellers are ethnic groups, thereby clarifying their protection under race legislation. However, New Travellers are not classed as an ethnic group; but under the legal definition they could be categorised as 'Gypsy' because they lead a nomadic lifestyle. Although a broad generalisation, it is possible to suggest that in legal cases referring to planning applications or appeals, the definition leans more heavily on the issue of nomadism; however, in cases examining harassment there is more of a tendency to use definitions relating to ethnicity. The Office of the Deputy Prime Minister (ODPM) has recognised the difficulties around the concept of 'settled' Travellers; and as part of its consultation on updating Circular 1/94 it mooted the following definition:

For the purposes of this Circular 'Gypsies and Travellers' means

A person or persons who have a traditional cultural preference for living in caravans and who either pursue a nomadic habit of life or have pursued such a habit but have ceased travelling, whether permanently or temporarily, because of the education needs of their dependent children, or ill-health, old age, or caring responsibilities (whether of themselves, their dependants living with them, or the widows and widowers of such dependents), but does not include members of an organised group of travelling show people or circus people, travelling together as such.

(Planning for Gypsy and Traveller Sites,
Consultation Paper, 2004: 11)

The problem of defining Gypsies and Travellers tends to tax academics and lawyers, more than the travelling community themselves. Gypsies and Travellers might suggest that they know perfectly well who they are and that they would benefit more from moving the debate forward and examining wider issues.

Another term used in the book is 'settled community'. Whilst it is recognised that 'settled community' is rather generalised, it does denote non-Gypsies. It is realised that the 'settled community' is not one cohesive whole, indeed many different communities reside in settled accommodation. However, for the purposes of allowing a distinction between Gypsies and Travellers, and non-Gypsies and Travellers, a term is necessary and 'settled community' is often used in the relevant literature. Members of the 'settled community' may also be called 'Gaujo' by Gypsies and Travellers (alternative spellings, such as 'Gorgio', are also used). Although this term does not occur much in the book, it should be explained that 'Gaujo' is the Gypsy term for non-Gypsies.

Understanding and Researching Gypsies and Travellers

Acton (1994) raises valid points about the study and understanding of Gypsies:

> The 'visitors' to Romani studies have used a bewildering array of sociological theories to incorporate Gypsies. The racist anthropology of the nineteenth century saw them as genetic primitives in our midst. More modern anthropology continues to see their culture as a cause of their situation rather than their history and situation as the root of their culture; even the 'culture of poverty' had a brief vogue. Functionalists have seen them as a 'middleman minority' with a particular specialised trading function (Lauwagie 1979). Marxists have seen them variously as sub- or lumpen-proletariat, while interactionists have seen them as hereditary deviants. These theories, whether macro or micro, or somewhere in the muddled Mertonian middle, are usually supported by an ethnography of some particular Gypsy group, and may offer some partial insight into that group; but they say nothing about Gypsies as a whole. (Acton, 1994: 25)

Acton summarises the research context around Gypsies and Travellers and he analyses the epistemology of researchers from Marxists to Functionalists. He also discusses a problem which is true of many areas of research — that of generalising about a diverse group. He discusses the fact that ethnography of some description is invariably used in case study groups and then the findings are widened out from that group to represent all Gypsies and Travellers. Acton states that this type of research is not representative and should not be seen as such. He raises the issue of differentiating between 'true' and 'untrue' Gypsies and Travellers in research:

Quite often when I tell people I have worked with Gypsies for 25 years, they bend their heads closer to mine and ask confidentially if I realise that only a few of them are 'real' Gypsies, as though they were in possession of some arcane secret which I might well not have come across. The residue of this particular inverted form of racism works particularly against New Age Travellers, as though they should be deprived of the right to travel because of some racial inauthenticity. (Acton, 1994: 27)

As stated earlier, this book discusses Gypsies and Travellers as a whole group and does not make a distinction between different groups. The notion of 'real' Gypsies is also discussed later on as one of the key themes in media discourse.

The problem of non-Gypsies and Travellers conducting research with false assumptions is highlighted by various academics, including Acton (1994). For example Weckmann (1998) provides a list of 'do's and don'ts' for researching Gypsies and Travellers in Finland. Heuss (2000) also sounds a warning about the research into Gypsies and Travellers and he moots a methodology for anti-Gypsyism research. He states that:

Anti-Gypsyism research must not posit the existing structures of prejudice as the primary cause for the persecution of Roma, or else they will retrospectively rationalise the irrationality of the historical forms of these antipathies. (Heuss, 2000: 63)

There are many ethical considerations for research into Gypsies and Travellers and I have endeavoured to approach the research for this book in an appropriate, thoughtful way.

Next Steps

There is a considerable amount of policy and practice research, in the subject area of Gypsies and Travellers. However, current research does not engage with theories of control or discourse. The intention of existing research, such as Niner (2003) is to provide policy advice to the government on how to improve accommodation on a practical level; its intention is not to engage with theories of control and discourse. Nevertheless, there is a place for research that does engage with this theory, as control is often implicitly taken as a given, with no attempt to focus on its nature. This book aims to take the next step and to discuss theories of control and discourse in order to expand the debate on Gypsies and Travellers.

Chapter Two

Gypsies and Travellers

Introduction

Gypsies and Travellers are a much discussed group. Often the public debate is based on a notion of 'Gypsy' that has little basis in fact, but is instead constructed and reconstructed through discourse. This chapter aims to provide a historical and legislative context and to examine the relevant literature.

'Estimates of the size of Britain's Traveller and Gypsy population vary. The Council of Europe has estimated it to be 300,000 (with 200,000 in settled housing).' (Crawley, 2004: 6). However, it should be noted that these numbers are estimates and there is no exact calculation of how many Gypsies and Travellers live in England, or indeed in Europe. The Office of the Deputy Prime Minister oversees a national bi-annual count of Gypsy and Traveller caravans, but this still does not allow for accurate data. Indeed, Niner (2004b) has provided advice to the Government on how the Gypsy Count can be improved. Estimations of the number of Gypsies and Travellers in Europe were exaggerated in media and political debate prior to the accession of the new countries to the European Union on May 1st 2004. Campaigns by newspapers such as the Express and the Daily Mail resulted in a government announcement which stated that migrants from the accession countries would not be able to claim welfare benefits for the first two years of residency, and those who were not in work would be sent back to their country of origin. This political announcement appeared to come as a direct result of the media anti-Gypsy campaign.

Gypsies and Travellers continue to face discrimination and harassment, despite the positive moves towards a more integrationist approach that affects other Black and Minority Ethnic groups. Extreme political parties, such as the British National Party, have their part to play; but so too does the media, the politicians and the general public. Crawley quoted CRE's Trevor Phillips at the launch of their Gypsy and Traveller Strategy in October 2003:

> The launch of this consultation is a major step forward for the CRE in trying to find out more about and act upon the appalling levels of discrimination faced by Gypsies and Travellers. For this group, Great Britain is still like the American Deep South for black people in the 1950's. Extreme levels of public hostility exist in relation to Gypsies and Travellers—fuelled in part by irre- sponsible media reporting of the kind that would be met with outrage if it was targeted at any other ethnic group. (Phillips quoted in Crawley, 2004: 2)

Gypsies and Travellers have gone through systems of control, discrimination, and harassment throughout their long and varied histories. Some of the current systems of control, in England, include:

- Legislation—Criminal Justice and Public Order Act 1994 which allows Gypsies to be moved on from unauthorised sites after 28 days.

- Local Policy—for instance the rules governing licences on authorised local authority sites are almost one-sided. Although all tenancy agreements have rules and regulations, the Gypsy site licences are strict and the onus is on the Gypsy to behave rather than the Local Authority to provide a good service.

- Lack of Authorised Sites—there is a shortage of authorised sites for Gypsies and Travellers, this means they have to camp on unauthorised sites or apply to the Local Authority as home- less and change their lifestyles to fit in with 'mainstream' hous- ing. This is often without adequate support that should accompany a major life change.

- Lack of Facilities on Authorised Sites—although this is improving on a lot of sites, some Gypsies and Travellers live on unsatisfactory sites (see Niner, 2003).

- Lack of Support for Gypsies and Travellers—the travelling life- style is not supported, it is not easy to administer welfare or support apart from according to geographical boundaries, and so the travelling population fall outside of this because they do not belong to a particular locality.

- Perceptions and Language—racist and bigoted language is used about Gypsies and Travellers and there are false assump- tions about the characteristics of Gypsies. There is also some- times a distinction between Gypsies and Travellers in this perception.

A Brief History

There is a variety of work which examines the history of Gypsies and Travellers in great depth; see Acton (1974, 1994 and 2000), Acton and Mundy (1997), Hancock (2002), Hawes & Perez (1996), Kenrick & Clark (1999), Mayall (1995), and Tong (1998).

Acton states that:

> The ancestors of the Romani-speaking peoples left India some one thousand years ago, moving along trade routes trodden over the centuries by countless other migratory nations. Some two or three hundred years later, contemporary documents attest their arrival in eastern Europe; before the end of the fifteenth century their presence is recorded in the British Isles. They brought with them a language whose Indian construction was in the eighteenth century to betray their history to the learned world; but with the Indian base came loan words from every country on their path; and hybridisation and creolisation with other languages has fragmented the Romani language into hundreds of dialects. Today, like the Jews, they live throughout the world, sometimes intermarrying, sometimes not, disunited politically, heterogeneous culturally, and with the most diverse aspirations. (Acton, 1974: 1)

The Roma arrived in Europe around 1300 and Kenrick and Clark (1999) note that the first authenticated records of a Gypsy presence in England was 1514 — in Lambeth. According to Kenrick and Clark's history, the Gypsies were welcomed by 'commoners' who had work that needed doing and who also wanted entertaining. The church objected to palmistry and fortune telling and the government was concerned that because they didn't live in a fixed abode then they were not easy to 'register' for details such as name and date of birth. This lack of governmental control is possibly one of the reasons for the state's treatment of Gypsies and Travellers still today. This is one of the central tensions in the relationship between both the state and Gypsies, and between non-Gypsies ('Gaujos') and Gypsies.

By 1530 the first piece of legislation expelling Gypsies was introduced by Henry VIII, this law also forbade the transportation of Gypsies into England — any Gypsy passengers were hanged. In 1540 the Gypsies were allowed to live under their own laws in Scotland but by 1541 the first Scottish anti-Gypsy laws were introduced. Edward VI brought in a law which required Gypsies to be branded with a 'V' (for vagabond) and enslaved for two years, escapees were branded with a 'S' and enslaved for life. In 1562 there was a further act relating to 'vagabonds' which meant that they didn't have to leave the country as long as they ceased their travelling lifestyle, all others who refused had to either leave the country or face execution. A similar law was passed in Scotland in 1573. The last known execution of a Gypsy took place in 1650; other Gypsies were banished to America. Deportation of Gypsies continued and some merchants were given permission to ship Gypsies to the Caribbean as slaves. In 1780 some of the anti-Gypsy laws started to be repealed, although not all. In 1822 the Turnpike Act was introduced, which meant that Gypsies camping on the roadside were fined (Patrin, 2000). During the Victorian era Gypsies and Travellers were certainly 'othered' in discourse (Holloway, 2002). 1908 saw the introduction of the Children's Act in England which made education compulsory for Gypsy children for half of the year; this was continued in the 1944 Education Act. During the Second World War the Nazis drew up a list of English Gypsies for internment and the holocaust of the Gypsies in Europe is well documented (Kenrick, 1999). However, the government in England did provide caravan sites for families of Gypsies either in the army or working the land, but unfortunately these camps were closed after the war—this contrasts with the 'homes fit for heroes' for non-Gypsy army men (Patrin, 2000).

Where there was an after-war effort, under a Labour government, to build 'homes fit for heroes' for the house dwelling English population, the Gypsies who had fought in the war came back to find that their caravan sites had been demolished by the police and their families had moved on to new places (Kenrick and Clark 1999). Despite the lack of provision for Gypsies and Travellers coming home from the war the Labour government aimed to demonstrate a more liberal, understanding approach to the Gypsy lifestyle and it was hoped that a network of Gypsy sites would be built. However, in 1960 under the Conservative government the Caravan Sites (Control of Development) Act prevented new private sites being built. In 1968, Harold Wilson's Labour government introduced the 1968 Caravan Sites Act which required local authorities to provide sites for Gypsies in England. Unfortunately, the Act was never fully enforced and the envisaged post-war network of sites did not come to fruition. By 1972, some local authorities were already exempt from building sites for caravans and finally in 1994, the Criminal Justice and Public Order Act undid any of the benefits of the Caravan Sites Act (1968) (Patrin, 2000).

Political and Legislative Context

There is much discussion of Gypsy/Traveller issues at a political level, yet there is still little evidence of political will to provide for them. The Office of the Deputy Prime Minister (ODPM) Planning, Local Government and the Regions Select Committee published their report on Gypsy and Traveller sites in November 2004. One of the main recommendations of the committee was that a legislative duty, for local authorities, to provide Traveller sites should be reintroduced.

The ODPM said it would respond fully to the report at a later date but added that the proposal was unlikely to be taken up:

> A duty to provide sites is not necessarily an appropriate solution. A duty has been tried before and often did not produce sufficient or appropriate provision. (Johnston, 2004: 4)

However, ODPM have still asked councils to provide extra sites in their good practice guide *Diversity in Equality and Planning* (March 2005). Commentators suggest this will not be possible without enforcing a duty (Hilditch, 2005). Additionally, local authorities should also adhere to the Homelessness Act (2002) and the Housing Act (2004), the latter of which requires an accommodation needs survey to be undertaken. The ODPM has already reprimanded one council in Brentwood (Inside Housing, 2005), for not including the needs of this group in their local development plans.

Housing providers need to make sense of their duties under a mixed raft of legislation. This is not easy within the current discourse, which is positive in some areas of the press (particularly the housing press) but extremely negative in the more popular press (see the Sun campaign in March, 2005). This discourse affects strategies for providing accommodation for Gypsies and Travellers. Therefore, there is a need to understand the discourse surrounding the group and to see how it can be controlling.

The lack of political will has been discussed by commentators such as Morris & Clements (2002). Politicians perceive that Gypsies and Travellers are an unpopular group and therefore do not want to be associated with them. Some work by Marston (2002), recognises this need of politicians to distance themselves from unpopular groups, in his research on anti-social tenants in Australia.

There is a variety of legislation that affects Gypsies and Travellers. Examples include the Caravan Sites Act (1968), the Criminal Justice and Public Order Act (1994), Circular 1/94, the Planning and Compensation Act (2004), the Homelessness Act (2002), the Anti-Social

Behaviour Act (2003), the attempted Traveller Law Reform Bill (2002), Circular 02/2005 on temporary stop notices and the Housing Act (2004).

Other pieces of legislation and guidance include the Race Relations Act (1976) and the Race Relations (Amendment) Act (2000) which places a duty on public authorities to stop unlawful discrimination. The Human Rights Act (1998) is also important because it legally enshrines the European Convention on Human Rights. In particular, Article 8 is referred to in case-law from the European Court in deciding Gypsy/Traveller cases. This article protects a person's right to respect for his private and family life and his home, and it prevents interference by a public body in exercising this right.

In addition to Circular 1/94, there are a range of other pieces of guidance, such as 18/94 on unauthorised camping. On planning issues, Planning Policy Guidance 1, 3, 12 and 18 cover strategic and operational issues. In February 2006 ODPM published a range of new guidance including Circular 1/2006 Planning for Gypsy and Traveller Sites. This will replace Circular 1/94.

Finally, before moving on to discuss legislation in more detail, it is necessary to mention the Gypsy Sites Refurbishment Grant, which was introduced in 2001. Although this is a positive move towards improving existing provision, it does not increase it. Indeed, there is evidence from Gypsies and Travellers, reiterated in the ODPM select committee report (November 2004) that during the improvement of sites, the number of pitches is actually reduced.

One of the main pieces of legislation affecting Gypsies and Travellers is the Criminal Justice and Public Order Act (CJPOA) (1994). Section 80 of the CJPOA repealed the Caravan Sites Act (1968). The Caravan Sites Act had made a duty on county councils to identify Gypsy/Traveller sites and on district councils to manage the sites. If local authorities provided sufficient sites then additional powers of eviction, from unauthorised encampments, were given. The take-up of the duties under the Caravan Sites Act (1968) was not as swift as had been anticipated and, despite an increase in provision for Gypsies and Travellers, it was not viewed as a success by central government when they debated the merits of the Criminal Justice and Public Order Act (1994). Crawley (2004) in discussing the Act, said that:

> ... perhaps most importantly, the Government was ideologically committed to the proposition that private enterprise – and specifically the purchasing of land by Travellers and Gypsies on

which to build their own sites—could satisfy the demand for accommodation. (Crawley, 2004: 19)

Partly because of this focus on private enterprise and self-help, by the Conservative government, there was a need for planning law provision to accommodate this. The Department of the Environment Circular 1/94 was supposed to meet the changing needs of the legislation applying to Gypsies and Travellers, this is discussed momentarily.

The Criminal Justice and Public Order Act (1994) also had practical, as well as ideological and political, implications for Gypsies and Travellers. One of the more prominently discussed sections of the Act is Section 61. Section 61 gave powers to the police to move Travellers on from unauthorised encampments. Although there were four criteria for moving Travellers on, the bar was set quite low and it was relatively easy to satisfy all four criteria. The first criterion of Section 61 was that two or more people were trespassing on land; secondly they were there with a purpose of residing there. The third criterion related to the owner of the land having first taken reasonable steps to ask the Travellers to leave. The fourth criterion was twofold; either damage had to have been done to the land or property, or abusive and threatening language had to be used; or there had to be more than six vehicles stopped on the land—it must be noted that when a vehicle is not driving on the highway and it has stopped, a van and a towing caravan are counted as two separate vehicles by the police. Despite these criteria seeming simple to satisfy, there are many comments amongst the public and the police that there are not enough legislative powers to deal with Gypsies and Travellers. It is possible that the police say this so that it is not seen to be their fault if there are Gypsies and Travellers on unauthorised encampments. Indeed the police do take different discretionary approaches to interpreting Section 61 throughout the country with some areas being much more accepting of unauthorised encampments, as long as there is no physical harm being done. New encampments may also settle on land that is owned by Gypsies and Travellers, in which case it is a matter to be referred to the planning authorities. Indeed, the government has published (March 2005) Circular 02/2005 which allows for Temporary Stop Notices to be put on unauthorised developments.

Circular 1/94 (DoE, 1994) attempted to focus on self-help and free enterprise on site provision for Gypsies and Travellers. It was later backed up by DoE guidance in 1998 *Managing Unauthorised Camping*

– *a good practice guide* (subsequently a revised edition was published in early 2004). Circular 1/94 had the intention of creating a level playing field for Travellers when they applied for planning permission to build a site on their own land. It states the main intentions are:

- to provide that the planning system recognises the need for accommodation consistent with gypsies' nomadic lifestyle;
- to reflect the importance of the plan-led nature of the planning system in relation to gypsy site provision, in the light of the Planning and Compensation Act 1991; and
- to withdraw the previous guidance indicating that it may be necessary to accept the establishment of gypsy sites in protected areas, including Green Belts.

(Circular 01/94, Gypsy Sites and Planning, DoE: 1)

The Circular refers to the planning and location of sites in local authority areas and it states that policies for site provision are vital in order to clarify the situation both for planners and for Gypsies and Travellers. With regard to planning applications, the Circular says (in bold writing to denote its importance):

Authorities should recognise that they may receive applications from gypsies without local connections which could not reasonably have been foreseen in their development plan policies. Authorities should not refuse private applications on the grounds that they consider public provision in the area to be adequate, or because alternative accommodation is available elsewhere on the authorities' own sites. (Circular 01/94: 5)

This part of the Circular encapsulates the self-help principle that was mooted by Crawley (2004) and it makes clear that planning applications from Gypsies and Travellers should be treated in the same vein as planning applications from members of the settled community. Unfortunately though, Circular 1/94 was not implemented in the spirit with which it was intended.

The experience of Travellers and Gypsies who do apply for planning permission is almost invariably that they are refused, forcing some families into long and protracted legal battles with no more likelihood of success than before Circular 1/94 was issued. Some families are deeply traumatised by these disputes as some authorities have used unfair tactics to defeat applications. (Crawley, 2004: 21)

This view is echoed by Morris (1998):

Statistics since 1991 indicate that the number of appeals diminished after Circular 1/94 was issued, and that the number allowed on appeal also reduced proportionately. Between 1991 and 1993 there were 248 appeals against refusals of applications, of which 67 were successful. From 1994 to 1996 there were only 140 appeals, of which 36 were allowed on appeal. This implies also that there were less applications. (Morris, 1998: 636)

The ODPM select committee report (November 2004) also recognised the problems of Circular 1/94. Evidence to the committee cited the lack of a coherent definition of Gypsies and Travellers as one of the causes. However, the committee felt that adding further definitions to those already in existence would only complicate matters. Regardless, ODPM consulted on a replacement for Circular 1/94, which includes a section on the definition of Gypsies and Travellers.

Gypsies and Travellers can be excluded from understanding their rights in law. However, appeals against planning decisions are made and this body of case-law provides some clarification; but there are still many inconsistencies. An example of this is in two planning appeal cases. The first was *Wrexham County Borough Council v National Assembly for Wales and Berry* (2003) EWCA Civ 835. In this case, the Court of Appeal set aside the High Court's decision to uphold Mr Berry's planning permission. The premise for the final refusal, by the Court of Appeal, was that Mr Berry was no longer a Gypsy as he didn't lead a nomadic lifestyle. The reason that he didn't travel was because he was too ill, but the court did not recognise the concept of a 'retired' Gypsy. They stated that because Berry was no longer nomadic he was no longer a Gypsy and thus planning permission was refused. The problem of definition was outlined in chapter one, and this case exemplifies how the issue manifests in the judgement of the courts.

The second case is that of *Basildon District Council v The First Secretary of State and Rachel Cooper* (2003) EWHC 2621 Admin. The local authority brought this case to the High Court to appeal planning permission that had been given in accordance with Gypsy status. The council argued that because Mrs Cooper had moved permanently onto a piece of land that she was no longer nomadic and therefore, no longer a Gypsy. With the Berry case as precedent, the council may have expected a successful outcome. However, Mrs Cooper argued that she couldn't travel all of the time because there were not enough sites to stop at, and that she only moved onto the land when she had been moved off the roadside. She maintained that she still travelled occasionally to sell goods at craft fairs during the summer. The court found in favour of Mrs Cooper because they agreed that she had been forced to give up her nomadic way of life because of a lack of sites. Although this case is similar to Berry, there is a distinction because the law will not recognise a 'retired' Gypsy, someone who does not travel at all because of ill health or through choice. However, in this case it recognised that Gypsies and Travellers are forced to give up their way of life through insufficient provision of accommodation.

Commentators on the legislation, as well as Gypsies and Travellers, have noticed that the powers to move Travellers on from unauthorised encampments has increased, whilst the duties on local authorities to provide Travellers' sites has decreased. In line with the confusion over planning legislation and case law it has been suggested by some that whilst over 80% of planning applications from the settled community are approved, 90% of applications from Gypsies and Travellers are refused (Bowers, 2004). The planning legislation for Gypsies and Travellers may improve with the revision of Circular 1/94. Additionally, the Planning and Compulsory Purchase Act (2004), offers an opportunity for strategic planning of sites in the regional spatial strategies. However, until there is evidence of the new Act being implemented, Gypsies and Travellers feel that the current planning legislation seems to disadvantage them. This scepticism is also shared by the ODPM select committee (November 2004). The committee stated that it was not convinced that the regional spatial strategies would result in an increased provision of sites, partly because provision of Gypsy/Traveller accommodation remains too political an issue. This planning problem has had the effect of making many Gypsies and Travellers homeless when, if given permission, they could have provided accommodation for themselves. There is an assumption of planning bias amongst the Traveller community, but more empirical research needs to be done in this area.

The Homelessness Act (2002) is another important piece of legislation for Gypsies and Travellers. The Act placed a duty on local authorities to think strategically about housing provision for homeless people and to be proactive in meeting the need. They were required to develop strategies that reviewed and predicted levels of homelessness and housing need in their area. Gypsies and Travellers are covered by the Housing Act (1996) which includes those who live in moveable structures, but who are not able to reside in them, in its definition of homelessness. Lord Avebury was concerned that the needs of Travellers were not being considered under homelessness legislation. Crawley (2004) summarises Avebury's findings:

> ... recently undertook a survey of 157 local authorities showing unauthorised encampments in the last bi-annual count of caravans. The survey looked at the authorities' Homelessness Strategies and whether Travellers were included within them. Eight authorities appear not to have produced strategies at all. Of the 137 authorities that did produce strategies, 72 per cent failed to make any reference to Travellers at all, despite having reported unauthorised encampments in the last bi-annual count. The research also found that there was no indication of any strategies for consultation with national or local Traveller organisations, or of advice being given by the authority's own Traveller or Gypsy officers. (Crawley, 2004: 11)

A recent example of case law which found in favour of homeless Gypsies and Travellers was the European Court of Human Rights case of *Connors v The United Kingdom (2004) (application no. 66746/01)*. The facts of the case are multi-faceted; but fundamentally, Connors and his extended family were evicted from a local authority site which they had lived on (with a short break away) for nearly fifteen years. The summary of the judgement was released by the Registrar of the European Court of Human Rights. In summing up, in relation to Article 8, it was said that:

> The court observed that the vulnerable position of gypsies as a minority meant that some special consideration had to be given to their needs and their different lifestyle both in the relevant regulatory framework and in reaching decisions in particular cases. To that extent, there was a positive obligation on the United Kingdom to facilitate a gypsy way of life.
> (http://press.coe.int/cp/2004/267a(2004).htm)

Connors had been evicted from the site because the local authority maintained there were issues of anti-social behaviour; however Connors was not given an opportunity to refute the allegations, he was just evicted. The European Court of Human Rights' judgement stated that there should be no reason why local authority sites would be unmanageable if they were required to establish reasons for evicting long-standing occupants. This judgement has since been translated, by the housing press, as giving Gypsies the same rights as tenants (Inside Housing, 2004: 8).

In conclusion, the European Court of Human Rights placed a responsibility, on the UK government, to facilitate a Gypsy way of life and it condemned the current policy regime:

> It would rather appear that the situation in England, as it had
> developed, for which the authorities had to take some responsi-
> bility, placed considerable obstacles in the way of gypsies pursu-
> ing an actively nomadic lifestyle while at the same time
> excluding from procedural protection those who decided to take
> up a more settled lifestyle.
>   (http://press.coe.int/cp/2004/267a(2004).htm)

If the Homelessness Act (2002) is implemented properly, and if strategies are drawn up in line with the Planning and Compensation Act
(2004) then the UK may come more in line with the European Court
of Human Rights' judgement of facilitating a Gypsy way of life.
Additionally, the duty to assess the accommodation needs of Gypsies and Travellers and include findings in local development plans
is contained in the Housing Act (2004). However, there is a long way
to go before results from these pieces of legislation may be seen.

A large amount of case-law, particularly in relation to planning
issues, hangs on understanding a definition of what a Gypsy/
Traveller is. Much of the evidence shows that definition is divided
between 'being' and 'doing' and it is linked to perceptions of 'real'
versus 'fake'. Indeed, the 'real' and the 'simulacrum' (Sandland,
1996) is enshrined in race relations legislation. The Commission for
Racial Equality (CRE) has confirmed that Gypsies and Irish Travellers are classed as racial groups and as such should be protected by
the Race Relations (Amendment) Act 2000. On the other hand New
Travellers are not classed as a racial group and are not afforded legislative protection from discrimination and harassment. This distinction seems to divide the 'genuine' and the 'simulacrum' along the
lines of being, rather than doing. New Travellers lead a nomadic lifestyle, and so according to the case-law, outlined earlier, could be
seen as Gypsy in the planning law. However, subsequent cases and
differing interpretations, both legislatively and politically, see the
New Traveller as even more 'other' than Gypsies and Irish Travellers, and they are not afforded protection from discrimination and
harassment as a group. Nevertheless, in other areas of the law, particularly planning legislation and its local application, the converse
is true. The essence of 'being' a Gypsy does not hold in a court of law
if the individual is no longer living a nomadic lifestyle; as was
discussed in relation to the Berry case earlier. It would appear that
for planning cases, nomadism is key; and for harassment cases,
ethnicity is the focus.

It is now necessary to turn, briefly, to the Anti-Social Behaviour
Act 2003. Crawley (2004) said: 'There is an unacceptable and persis-

tent culture of linking anti-social behaviour and the accommodation needs of Travellers and Gypsies.' (pg 13) and this is evidenced in the Anti-Social Behaviour Act 2003. Part Seven of the Anti-Social Behaviour Act contains provisions which can be interpreted to move Travellers on from unauthorised encampments, where a local authority can show that official sites are provided. The Anti-Social Behaviour Act 2003 is important because it embodies what Crawley objects to — the 'unacceptable' link between anti-social behaviour and Gypsies and Travellers. To some extent the issues around sites are dealt with on a strategic level in the Planning and Compensation Act (2004) and the Housing Act (2004), but on a practical level local authorities will be consulting the Anti-Social Behaviour Act (2003). If the Government and the judiciary continue to make these unacceptable links then there is limited chance for members of the public to break the perceived link between anti-social behaviour and Gypsies and Travellers.

The Traveller Law Reform Bill (2002) warrants discussion here, although it has since failed, due to lack of time in the parliamentary session. It proposed the establishment of a Gypsy and Traveller Accommodation Commission to promote equality of opportunity for Gypsies and Travellers, to monitor site provision and to examine unauthorised encampments and any associated anti-social behaviour. The Bill also included a duty to facilitate site provision through exercising powers under the Caravan Sites and Control of Development Act (1960) and it debated funding issues — for instance grants for education and Housing Corporation funding for caravan site construction.

The primary legislation and case law affecting Gypsies and Travellers is varied and complex. The issue has been included here by way of an introduction to the problems faced by the group.

Literature Review

In addition to providing a historical and political/legislative context, this chapter includes a brief literature review of published academic work in this field. Some key themes in the published research include:

- 'Real' versus 'fake' (Shuinear, 1997 and Stewart, 1997)
- Political prejudice (Hawes and Perez, 1996)
- Need for more and better sites (Niner, 2003)
- Invisibility of Gypsies in policy (Morris, 2003)

- Cost of Gypsies (Morris and Clements, 2002)
- Neighbours' views (Duncan, 1996)
- Recommendations for the future (Crawley, 2004 and ODPM Select Committee, 2004)

Some of these themes are echoed in the themes from my research, outlined in Figure two, Chapter One.

There is no doubt that Gypsies and Travellers have been subject to racism, discrimination and even execution. Approximately 500,000 Gypsies and Travellers were executed in the Nazi holocaust and they are sometimes seen as the forgotten victims of this era. One publication which analyses the Gypsies in the Holocaust is *In the shadow of the Swastika* (Kenrick, 1999). More recently, it has been reported (McLaughlin, 2005) that Gypsy women in the Czech Republic continue to undergo forced sterilisation. It is important to highlight the strength of discrimination that Gypsies and Travellers have faced. This spectrum of discrimination—from negative discourse to execution—demonstrates the different steps outlined in Bauman's (1989) theory of proximity, which is analysed further on, in the theoretical framework.

Again, linked to Bauman's (1989) theory, and the need of the settled community to see Gypsies and Travellers as 'other', Shuinear (1997) discusses 'Gaujo' images of Gypsies and Travellers. She says in her chapter entitled *Why do Gaujos hate Gypsies so much, anyway?*:

> I want to put it even more precisely: just as Santa Claus is the idea of Christmas cheer and giving all rolled into one fairytale person —their *personification*—Gaujos need Gypsies to *personify* their own faults and fears, thus lifting away the burden of them.
>
> This need is so overpowering that time after time, in place after place, Gaujos create situations forcing Gypsies to fill this role.
>
> It is important to remember that what we're talking about here are not 'alien' faults and problems but *Gaujo's own*; therefore, the people onto whom these are projected must clearly distinct from the Gaujo mainstream, but not utterly foreign to it: just as in cinema, the screen must be neither too close nor too distant if the image projected onto it is to remain sharply focused.

(Shuinear, 1997: 27)

What Shuinear seems to say is that the identity of Gypsies and Travellers is not based on fact but is instead dependent on the projection of a given image from the settled community—the Gaujos. The fairytale image of the 'true' Gypsy is positive, much more in the vein of Shuinear's Santa Claus. The 'fake' Traveller is a negative projected image and is seen to apply to many more people. This is because the rosy image of the 'true' Gypsy (as with Santa Claus) is not seen in reality, and therefore all Gypsies and Travellers become stereotyped by the projected image of the 'fake' Gypsy or Traveller.

Stewart (1997) discusses Gypsies and Travellers in a more fixed and abstract way, he refers to a persona which is not challenged, as it is by Shuinear (1997), but is accepted as truth. He examines how they have managed to keep their identity throughout societal changes and without a nation state:

> Every age, ours as much as its predecessors, believes that it will be the last to be blessed (and cursed) by the presence of the Gypsies. Well-wishers and hostile commentators, romantics and cynics alike are of fixed opinion that the 'wanderers of the world' have at last been 'domesticated', their way of life finally out-moded and that 'the time of the Gypsies' has run out. Such asser-tions like many made about Gypsies are based on no more than casual acquaintance with the realities of Gypsy life. In truth Gypsies all over Europe have been remarkably successful in preserving their way of life, adapting to their changed conditions in order to remain the same. (Stewart, 1997: 84)

Stewart refers to changing trades as an example of the adaptation of the Gypsy and Traveller identity. He says that second-hand car deal-ing has replaced horse trading, fortune telling has replaced wooden-peg making and building has replaced the work of blacksmiths. However, to assume that Gypsies and Travellers belong to particu-lar trades is stereotyping. It is important to remember that there is no homogenous identity of the travelling community; they can be as heterogeneous as the settled community.

Hawes and Perez (1996) provide a history of Gypsies and Travel-lers, which is important because of its discussion on 'the politics of prejudice'. They look at how issues in the planning system and in defining Gypsies and Travellers, conspire to prejudice them. Hawes and Perez quote one Traveller's perception of this prejudice:

> In the words of one Traveller, it is as if the Gorgio is saying:

> 'Of course we must cater for your interesting differences, but we must encourage you, to the point of coercion, to stop being different—or at least make it as difficult as possible.'

> (Hawes and Perez, 1996: 156)

Niner (2002, 2003 and 2004a) has provided the most recent research into the needs of Gypsies and Travellers in England. Her report *Local Authority Gypsy/Traveller Sites in England* (2003) covers a wide range of issues and includes a variety of different studies. A survey of local authorities was conducted to establish existing Gypsy/Traveller accommodation issues for local authorities, and a surveyor was employed to examine the condition of local authority sites. Niner reports on site management and site finances, including the views of Gypsies and Travellers on tenure and licence fees. Their views are included in the report, which were the result of a series of interviews with Gypsies and Travellers across a range of sites. The obstacles to new site provision, referred to in Niner's report (2003: 205-6) include a summary of some of the still pertinent issues raised in the Cripps (1977) report *Accommodation for Gypsies: A report on the workings of the Caravan Sites Act 1968*. This report examined the success of the Caravan Sites Act 1968 and found that unsatisfactory progress had been made due to a number of obstacles.

Niner refers to five of the Cripps report obstacles. First, is the importance of public opinion (I examined discourse from the media, politicians and the public for this book in the light of this obstacle). Secondly, Gypsy habits were referred to by Cripps (1977). Niner clarifies that this is in relation to the anti-social behaviour of a minority, which forms the perception of the settled community of all Gypsies and Travellers. Vandalism was a third obstacle, the vandalism of some of the sites made councils less willing to refurbish them or carry on providing them — one could also consider the problem of fly-tipping here; although, it must be stressed that Gypsies and Travellers are not solely responsible for fly-tipping on or near sites, but they are perceived to be. A fourth concern for Cripps (1977) and Niner (2003) was the idea of Gypsy/Traveller site provision being a national responsibility; this may have led to some local authorities feeling it was not their concern and therefore not directing resources to the issue. This idea links in with a principle discussed throughout the book, that of Bauman's (1989) theory of proximity. The notion of its being a national responsibility meant that the local authorities could put a distance between themselves and the needs of the locality. Finally, the last obstacle Niner (2003) quotes from Cripps (1977), is the idea that the problem of Gypsy/Traveller provision is uncertain. This is most certainly still relevant today with many local authorities and national organisations being unable to confirm the level and depth of Gypsy/Traveller needs; these needs are not just related to accommodation but also particularly health and education. The nomadism of some Gypsies and Travellers makes it difficult for local providers to plan service delivery. Niner backed up the obstacles quoted from Cripps with evidence from the local authority survey conducted for her report (2003). The main obstacles, in order of the frequency with which they were identified by local authorities were:

Resistance from local residents	89%
Funding for new sites	76%
Problems getting planning permission	64%
Lack of suitable land for sites	51%
Inadequate commitment from Government	50%
Inadequate commitment locally	50%
Lack of a duty	48%
Funding for maintaining existing sites	31%
Other	8%

(Niner, 2003: 206)

It is interesting to note that the obstacle of 'lack of a duty' is comparatively low down the list. Reformers, such as the Traveller Law Reform Coalition, suggest that a change in the law is what is needed to increase the provision of sites for Gypsies and Travellers. However, the Niner (2003) evidence from local authorities suggests that energies should be focused on reducing the resistance from local residents – perhaps through increased understanding between the settled and travelling communities – and on increased funding for site provision. Niner (2004a) recognises this need, in an examination of her findings, she says:

> Beyond and beneath this there is a clear task of educating the settled communities about Gypsies and Travellers, their cultures and lifestyles. To date, attitudes towards Gypsies/Travellers as a minority group seem to have concentrated mostly on segregation (onto sites, mostly hidden away and out of sight) with little social contact between Travelling and settled communities, or assimilation (fear of harassment can lead housed Gypsies/Travellers to hide their origins and abandon their traditional lifestyle). It is time to move towards an approach of integration where Gypsy/Traveller culture is understood and celebrated alongside that of other minorities in an ethnically diverse, multi-cultural Britain. (Niner, 2004a: 156)

Niner (2004b) also reports on the review of the Gypsy caravan count system. One of the flaws identified in the current bi-annual count is the lack of connectivity between the count and the policies and strategies on Gypsies and Travellers. This was one of the barriers highlighted in Niner (2003) particularly as the problem of sites is seen as 'national' and local authorities do not engage with the local levels of need. There is a sense that the count information should be for local authorities, rather than central government, as it is the local authorities who need to deliver the services on the ground.

A report conducted by the Cardiff Law School, (Thomas and Campbell, 1992) also looked at the current context of provision of Gypsy/Traveller sites, but this time it focused on Wales. It was not as wide ranging as the Niner (2003) report but it did question Gypsies and Travellers and other organisations on the current provision of sites and also asked how they felt about living in settled accommodation. The findings seemed to echo those in the Niner (2003) report and, in relation to living in settled accommodation, some Gypsies and Travellers felt they had to live in houses because there was little or no alternative provision; but as soon as there was they would leave their houses and move back onto sites.

Other important research in the area of Gypsies and Travellers includes Morris (1999) who looks at the invisibility of Gypsies and Travellers. Her notion of invisibility would seem, at first, to juxtapose the premise in this book that Gypsies and Travellers are made to be more visible because of their 'otherness'. However, Morris does not argue that Gypsies and Travellers are entirely invisible, but instead that their needs are invisible. She examines key literature in areas such as health and the environment. In health literature it was found that Gypsies and Travellers were not included in mainstream NHS documents. For instance the high mortality rate of Gypsy babies was not included in the discussion on the mortality rates of other BME infants. Morris (2003) included evidence in the form of views from politicians, professionals and Gypsies and Travellers. The lack of inclusion of Gypsies and Travellers in 'mainstream' policies and practices is backed up by other authors, such as Crawley (2004) who recommends that their accommodation needs are incorporated into mainstream housing legislation. This book argues that Gypsies and Travellers are made visible through discourse on their 'otherness' but would concur that their needs, such as the provision of sites, health and education services, remain invisible to policy makers and implementers. Indeed, Morris (1999) sums up this 'otherness' in relation to her discussion of excluding the ethnic group 'Gypsies' from the census:

> It is saddening, then, that the Office for National Statistics has refused to include, yet again, 'Gypsy' as a category in the 'Ethnic group questions' of the 2001 national census. They have said that it is open to Gypsies to tick the box entitled 'other' if they wish to

do so. Gypsies and Travellers are, indeed, 'other' and it appears that they will continue to be treated as such for some time to come, if they are noticed at all. (Morris, 1999: 403)

Morris and Clements published two books of interest, the first (1999) was a collection of papers entitled *Gaining Ground: Law Reform for Gypsies and Travellers* and the second (2002) was called *At What Cost? The economics of Gypsy and Traveller encampments.* Both publications are important in providing context to the current debate on issues facing Gypsies and Travellers; the latter publication is of interest because it examines the cost of not providing Gypsy/Traveller sites. Morris and Clements argue that cost was one of the reasons that the duty to provide sites was taken away and yet they say that no financial appraisal was undertaken to support this view. Their research surveyed local authorities for the costs resulting from the under-provision of Gypsy/Traveller sites; however they warn that the quantification of costs does not account for the suffering of Gypsies and Travellers:

> Why is the widespread myth that Gypsies and other Travellers do not pay tax or rent so often repeated? Why does the media constantly dwell on the costs of clearing unauthorised sites and no other contextual issues?
> Although the full answer to these questions may lie beyond the remit of this book, the intrinsic danger should form a backdrop to the subsequent analysis — for it is at least arguable that the language of cost in this context is the language of intolerance. It may be that as a society we count the cost of that which we do not value. That by constantly recording the cost of accommodating Travelling People we are articulating a racist and rhetorical question — namely whether we can afford them; that the sum total of Travelling cultures can be expressed in negative financial terms. (Morris and Clements, 2002: 2)

The idea that the language of cost is also one of intolerance is interesting. The concept links in strongly with my findings. One of the strongest areas of discourse in the analysis of media reporting, and in public speech, is the issue of cost, particularly in relationship to cleaning up mess. The idea of cost as part of a negative language is discussed further on, but it is interesting to note the links with Morris and Clements' research here. Morris (2001) discusses costs, in a similar vein, but this time in relation to the zero-tolerance policing policies in some areas. She challenges the notion that zero-tolerance is as cost effective as is supposed by local and police authorities.

One of the recent publications looking at the issues facing Gypsies and Travellers is by Crawley (2004). *Moving Forward, the provision of accommodation for Travellers and Gypsies* was published by the Institute of Public Policy Research (IPPR). It was produced in consultation with a number of Gypsies and Travellers and relevant organisations. The report helped to provide a position statement, of sorts, on what research had been undertaken, how recent and currently drafted legislation would affect Gypsies and Travellers; and it provided recommendations. The report examined the policy and legislation which currently governs this issue and it highlighted problems with monitoring need (the report was published before Niner (2004b) which provided recommendations on improving the Gypsy caravan count). Amongst the key conclusions, it was stated that:

> ... it is clear that at all levels of the political spectrum there is a lack of political will to tackle the marginalisation of Travellers and Gypsies in society and to address the impact that this has both on these communities and on those local authorities who are expected to provide support without any additional resources or political leadership from central government. The discourse is one of enforcement and eviction rather than provision, and Travellers and Gypsies are viewed by many as a problem rather than a social group in need of support. Underlying this is a failure to accept the nature of the nomadic life style and provide services which suit it. (Crawley, 2004: 55)

The discourse of the media, politicians and public is one which highlights the cost and problems of Gypsies, rather than their needs. The specific recommendations of the IPPR report referred to the need for Gypsy/Traveller sites to be classed as housing, and asked generally for Gypsy/Traveller issues to be mainstreamed into housing policy and legislation (rather than marginalised in Anti-Social Behaviour legislation). Provision for sites should be included in regional spatial strategies and funding provided through regional housing boards; local authorities should be *required* to make provision for sites and these sites should be run by local authorities, registered social landlords or other bodies and that there should be a specialised national or regional social landlord to oversee this. In order to engage with central government, the report recommended that a top-level unit be created within the Office of the Deputy Prime Minister (ODPM) and that the unit should be advised by a representative 'Traveller Task Force'. The inclusion of Gypsies and Travellers in equal opportunities policies and standards, and housing strategies, was also highlighted as important (Crawley, 2004: 57).

The ODPM select committee produced a report in November, 2004, which reiterated a lot of Crawley's recommendations, including the Task Force. Their headline recommendation was to reintroduce the duty to provide sites, but ODPM rejected these proposals. They have, however, set up the Gypsy/Traveller Unit within ODPM during 2005.

There are a small number of research papers which deal with the issue of discourse and Gypsies and Travellers, and are relevant to the literature review here. Firstly, Erjavec (2001) examines the representation of the Roma of Slovenia in the media. Second, Leudar and Nekvapil (2000) look at how Czech Romanies are presented in television debates. Turner's (2000) paper *Gypsies and Politics in Britain*, examines the treatment of Gypsies in politics and this includes an analysis of some of the things that Jack Straw has said about Gypsies. Turner looks at the labelling of 'true' and 'untrue' and he makes comparisons with other ethnic minorities. I also make this comparison, later on, particularly with asylum seekers and some of their treatment in the media. Additionally, the words 'Gypsy' and 'Traveller' are examined from a Gypsy/Traveller perspective and there are differences of opinion amongst the travelling community on preferred labels. Turner then briefly analysed 'custom, belief and tradition' and drew a parallel with the Sikhs; this was an attempt to examine a definition of Gypsy in cultural and ethnic terms. Another relevant paper is also by Turner (2002) and is entitled *Gypsies and British Parliamentary Language: An Analysis*. This paper looks specifically at the language used in political debate in Britain and it finds the juxtaposition of the romantic Gypsy and the 'dirty' Traveller is present in the debate.

Clark and Campbell (2000) examine discourse, in the English media in 1997, which proposed that there was an 'invasion' of Czech Romany Gypsies. This was a selective investigation of newspapers over a two-week period. Helleiner and Szuchewycz (1997) describe an elite discourse in the Irish press, which legitimates coercive practices against Gypsies and Travellers.

These papers are discussed, further on, in the examination of discourse, in chapter five.

Conclusion

This chapter has outlined a brief history of Gypsies and Travellers to provide context for the remainder of the book. It has also provided a summary of the recent legislative climate. A range of research publications has been examined. Whilst there is up-to-date information on the issues, namely Niner (2003) and Crawley (2004), the focus has been on the practical measures that can be taken. I intend to take the debate on and to examine issues in a theoretical context. The next chapter will outline the theoretical framework. This will be followed by a deeper analysis of the three main areas of the framework: control, discourse, and society's need to 'other' particular groups such as Gypsies and Travellers.

Chapter Three

Developing a Theoretical Framework

Introduction

I suggest that discourse can be used to control Gypsies and Travellers, and themes from my research support this notion. However, there needs to be a theoretical underpinning to this supposition and the framework helps to outline this. Fundamentally, there are three elements to the framework: what controls Gypsies, how this is achieved, and why. Each element is examined in detail in the four following chapters.

Existing Theoretical Frameworks

There is an existing body of work which examines frameworks of control or discursive frameworks; for instance Akerstrom Anderson (2003) and Clegg (1989). Akerstrom Anderson discusses frameworks, within which to understand the myriad discourses in the social science field. He looks at four main theorists for their discursive frameworks, but the one to note here is Foucault. In summarising his understanding of Foucault, Akerstrom Anderson says:

> Power is present in our approach to others insofar as, for example, 'criminals', 'mad people' or 'sick people' are not in and of themselves criminal, mad or sick. Conversely, criminality and illness are discursive positions, which are established with the intent to control. (Akerstrom Anderson, 2003: 3)

Akerstrom Anderson groups four main areas of Foucault's work into an analytical strategy—he incorporates archaeological discourse analysis, genealogy, self-technology analysis and dispositive analysis. In addition he adds concepts from Koselleck, Laclau and Luhmann in order to provide a tabular framework in which to provide an extensive choice of discursive explanations.

Clegg (1989) draws on a large number of theorists, amongst them Foucault, in order to develop his framework of power. The conclusion of his research culminates in a diagrammatic framework explaining 'circuits of power'. Foucault is important in understanding the circuit, his notion of power as moving, rather than fixed, is a vital component of this idea. In explaining his diagrammatic framework, Clegg states:

> Power at this level will invariably be accompanied by resistance, which is indicated ... in the model of episodic power relations. Power which proceeds at the level of these episodic power relations is the most apparent, evident and economical circuit of power. (Clegg, 1989: 215)

Resistance to power is outlined by Clegg. This concept, and the circular notion of power, is discussed in chapter four of the present book. In constructing his framework, Clegg (1989) hangs his notion of power on ideas of modern and post-modern explanations of the state, organisation and the market. My framework focuses on Foucault's theory of gaze and links this with explanations of discourse. A further component of the framework is an analysis of society, norms and folk devils. This is in an attempt to explain why control of Gypsies and Travellers, through discourse, is seen as necessary in society. Neither Akerstrom Anderson (2003) nor Clegg (1989) tackle this issue; they concentrate on the how, rather than the why. Clegg states as much in his work:

> The circuits of power framework enables us to analyse how this is so. Why it should be so is another question, suited to more polemical occasions than this text allows. (Clegg, 1989: 272)

The question of why, is of great importance to my research. In failing to understand the motive for exercising a particular type of power and control, it is not possible to fully comprehend the concept of power. There is also a link between the motive behind power and the question of who is controlling and who is being controlled. Attached to this is the notion of who the controlling is for; this is not as simple as looking at who is doing the controlling. For instance, the government would deny that social control is to directly benefit them and allow for political shifts. Instead, they may suggest that it is for the benefit of the collective 'whole' of society. This is discussed in further detail later, but it is important to note that the 'why' and 'who' of control are developed, in this framework, in order to build on the work of authors, such as Akerstrom Anderson and Clegg, and to bridge a gap in this area of research.

Developing the Theoretical Framework

Three main theoretical areas will be discussed in detail, later in the book: control (Foucault's gaze), theories of discourse (and the links between theories on discourse and control) and, thirdly, theories on society, norms and folk devils (Bauman, 1989 and Cohen, 1980). The latter theory can be linked to explanations from researchers such as Shuinear (1997), outlined in chapter two. These theories propose a functionalist type of perspective, that a group such as Gypsies and Travellers is needed to take the burden of society's fears and faults. This begins to provide a motive for the control of the group through discourse and begins to answer the question of why there is a perceived need for the control of Gypsies and Travellers.

The framework brings together these three key areas:

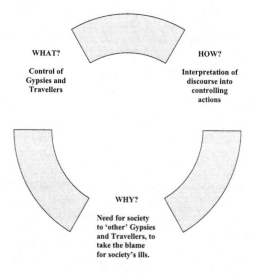

WHAT?

Control of Gypsies and Travellers

HOW?

Interpretation of discourse into controlling actions

WHY?

Need for society to 'other' Gypsies and Travellers, to take the blame for society's ills.

Figure 3: Theoretical Framework

The diagram shows three stages of a circular route of power and control: what, how and why. It is circular, rather than linear, because there is no set start and end point. Additionally, there are no arrows to denote direction of the route, as it is multi-directional and can flow any way.

The theoretical framework of this research, shown in figure three, hypothesises that surveillant control is exercised through discourse, because a particular group is seen to differ from macro societal norms. The controlled group, in this case, is Gypsies and Travellers. The framework could be applied to any group—asylum seekers, anti-social youths and so on. Indeed, examples of media reporting draw parallels between Travellers and asylum seekers—particularly in the discourse of 'real' versus 'fake'. The theoretical framework could be equally applied to any of them, as groups controlled through discourse.

It is important to remember that discourse is not just a matter of text and talk, it is not reactive but indeed productive and constructive. It is the translation of discourse into action that controls Gypsies and Travellers. For instance, the discourse of legislation and policy is translated into judgement and procedure. The outcome of these judgements and procedures has a real affect on whether Gypsies and Travellers can stay on a particular site, whether they can build a site on their own land, or indeed what services they can expect to receive in a particular local authority area. The legislative and policy discourse does not stop with the words on a page; it is the translation of the discourse into action that is controlling.

Discourse does not just reflect or describe a particular person or group, instead there is a process of definition and re-definition through discourse. For example, Berger and Luckmann (1966) discuss the social construction of reality, as broken into subjective and objective reality. Figure three, above, showed the circular notion of power in my theoretical framework, and this also reflects the definition and redefinition of objective and subjective reality. This is especially true when one looks at the question of who is being controlled. Gypsies and Travellers are defined according to societal norms and then kept under surveillance through societal discourse which controls and re-defines the group according to new subjective realities. This subjective reality is then taken as a new objective reality and so the definition and redefinition, through discourse, continues. During a discussion on Radio Four (2004), one of the examples of the impact of media discourse was of residents near Dover discussing asylum seekers according to the labels given to them in the media. When asked for examples of these asylum seekers in real life, the residents could not provide any. However, the subjective reality of the media discussion had become the objective reality of the Dover residents. The same could be seen in my analysis of media

reporting, and of the public's views (from the local authority planning consultation on the issue of labelling Gypsies and Travellers).
These two parts of the construction of discourse around Gypsies and
Travellers (1. the media and 2. the public) define and redefine the
group beyond the recognition of Gypsies and Travellers themselves.
This circularity of controlling discourse is demonstrated in figure
three.

The motivation of government and the media to define and redefine 'other' groups is examined later. Cohen (1980) analyses the need
for government to move a general fear into something more tangi-
ble, in order to allow for political shifts. It is possible to see the policies of former Home Secretary Blunkett (post 9/11) reflect this. The
fear of terrorist attack is heightened by government rhetoric in order
that policy and legislative shifts can be made under the guise of protecting the population. A similar motive can be found for the government in their discourse around Gypsies and Travellers. By othering
them, particularly on the issue of cost, the theory of proximity
(Bauman, 1989) means the general population is less concerned with
adverse treatment of them.

The motive for the media 'othering' Gypsies and Travellers is perhaps not as clear as that of the Government. However, one suggestion is that by perpetuating the stereotype of Gypsies and Travellers
as 'folk-devil' it enables more newspapers to be sold (and thus the
link with cost as motive is further enforced). This issue is discussed
elsewhere in the book, particularly in relation to the Express campaign to stop Roma from the EU accession countries claiming benefits in the UK. The theoretical element is also discussed in chapters
five and six, where Galtung and Ruge's (1973) news values are
examined. In perpetuating the discourse around Gypsies and Travellers the media is heightening their news value, which sells more
newspapers. The more 'other' Gypsies and Travellers are seen to be,
the more the population wants to read about them, the news then
'others' them even more and so the cycle continues.

Using the Framework

The theoretical framework was developed using the discussions and
conclusions in the following four chapters; and it enables some of the
concepts such as power, control, gaze and discourse to be
operationalised in the analysis of the empirical material. It is used as
a context within which to analyse the legislation, policy and practice

affecting Gypsies and Travellers; and the discourse surrounding
and controlling the group.

The theory outlines what type of power and control is being used
(surveillance/gaze), how it is being used (through discourse) and
why it is being used (to 'other' those that don't conform to societal
norms). It provides a vital link between the theoretical discussion
and the analysis of empirical data.

Not only does the theoretical context help to explain the practical
findings of the research, but in applying the theory it is possible to
conclude which theories are the most use in explaining certain phe-
nomena. Thus, the framework was not developed in isolation and
then applied to the findings, but the two parts of the research helped
to define one another. In operationalising key concepts such as gaze
and discourse in the explanation of the media analysis, public
speech analysis and Gypsy/Traveller focus groups. It was possible
to see, for instance, that Foucault's gaze was particularly important
in explaining the findings of the research. Although his ideas on
governmentality were vital in defining what is meant by power and
control, particularly in chapter four, it was his notion of the gaze
which was prevalent in analysing the discursive control over Gypsies and Travellers.

The theoretical framework, in this brief chapter, has brought
together key theoretical concepts (gaze, discourse and society) to
provide a link between theory and my research findings. It has built
upon the work of writers, such as Clegg (1989) and Akerstrom
Anderson (2003) in providing an explanation of why power is exercised over certain groups. It has also analysed who (which particular
groups) are part of those controlling and those being controlled. But,
it has been explained that because of the fluid notion of power, the
circular route of the framework (as depicted in figure 3) is multi-
directional. The following chapter looks, in much more detail, at
explanations of power and control and focuses on the work of
Foucault.

Chapter Four

Theories of Control

Introduction

This chapter takes a theoretical approach to understand how control in society is achieved. Many academics and authors have tried to define power and control and to explain how it works and who has got it. This chapter aims to examine existing theories of control in order to understand the type of control that is used over Gypsies and Travellers. The literature consists of a large body of work. In order to make sense of it, I start by looking at Lukes' (1974) typology of power which uses three main classifications. The chapter is ordered in this way so that it is possible to see how descriptions of power have changed and developed. It will culminate in an analysis of the work of Foucault, including a critique of his theories, in order to explain the links between control and discourse.

There is a trend in the descriptions; in the main they start off with a Machiavellian description of zero-sum power with force used to discipline and enforce control, this is what Lukes describes as a traditional type of power and control. They end with theorists such as Garland (2001), Rose (1999) and Dandeker (1990) drawing on themes of relational power as mooted by Foucault (1980). These types of power have gone beyond the middle-way and are indeed multi-directional — according to Lukes (1974).

The emphasis in this chapter is on Foucault, who is used frequently in modern discussions on power, and has some useful paradigms in which to discuss the meaning of power and control. Foucault is a reference point because of his explanations of discourse and the gaze, which can be applied to the control of Gypsies and Travellers. However, it must be remembered that Foucault is not the start point, or the end point, in discussions of control — which is why this chapter tries to put his work in the context of other thinkers in the subject.

Theories of Control in Context

Lukes (1974) discusses different dimensions of power and shows that there are three different classifications of control. He uses, as a starting point, a critique of the 'pluralist' one-dimensional definition of power plus a further critique of Bachrach and Baratz's (1970) two-dimensional definition of power. His own explanation of what power means takes a further three-dimensional view. Lukes summarises the differences between these different dimensions:

One Dimensional View of Power

Focus on   (a) behaviour

              (b) decision-making

              (c) (key) issues

              (d) observable (overt) conflict

              (e) (subjective) interests, seen as policy preferences revealed by political participation.

Two Dimensional View of Power

(Qualified) critique of behavioural focus

Focus on   (a) decision-making and non decision-making

              (b) issues and potential issues

              (c) observable (overt or covert) conflict

              (d) (subjective) interests, seen as policy preferences or grievances

Three Dimensional View of Power

Critique of behavioural focus

Focus on   (a) decision-making and control over political agenda (not necessarily through decisions)

              (b) issues and potential issues

              (c) observable (overt or covert) and latent conflict

              (d) subjective and real interests

(Lukes, 1974: 25)

Lukes' three dimensional view of power and his critique of the two preceding views on power, help to show the development of the arguments of power. The first view is quite simplistic and can draw parallels with the early theorists who used conflict as a focus—such as Machiavelli (1961). The second view is a critique of the first and does help to develop the argument by looking at the issue of non-decision making. However, it is the third which is the most useful for this book.

The three-dimensional view of power is the type where conflict is not necessary for power to exist. Indeed this strongest type of power is so effective because it is not noticed.

> ... is it not the supreme and most insidious exercise of power to prevent people, to whatever degree, from having grievances by shaping their perceptions, cognitions and preferences in such a way that they accept their role in the existing order of things, either because they can see or imagine no alternative to it, or because they see it as natural and unchangeable, or because they value it as divinely ordained and beneficial? (Lukes, 1974: 24)

It is the third dimension which allows for a wider sociological perspective on the examination of power. Lukes does highlight some difficulties in studying the three-dimensional approach (pages 50–51), particularly in relation to the problem of studying the exercise of power. These include inaction (how does one study something which is not observable?), unconscious decision making (if the person exercising control unconsciously is not aware of it then how is it observable to researchers?), and thirdly there is a problem because power and control can be exercised by groups and not just individuals (in observing a group how is it possible to identify the precise mechanisms of the exercise of power? It is not simply examining the exercise of power of individual A over B which is easier to analyse for causal power relationships). Lukes does state that these problems are not insurmountable, but instead that the researcher needs to be aware of their existence.

In order to exemplify the three dimensions further, a range of literature is examined and an attempt has been made to classify the literature according to the most appropriate dimension that it examines.

One and Two-Dimensional Views of Power

Machiavelli wrote his book *The Prince* towards the end of the 15th century. His advice to future Princes on how to obtain and keep power, bases itself on a mixture of virtue (it is made clear in the translation by Bull [1961] that this is the old sense of the word — cunning, guile, bravery, ruthlessness and determination) and luck. Power according to Machiavelli is a zero-sum entity that is won and lost, often through the use of force and deceit. This explanation of power may have been suitable for Italian religious leaders and politicians in the 15th century but it is not appropriate as an explanation of control for this chapter. The reason for including Machiavelli here is that his zero-sum notion is a simplistic approach to power and it fits in with a one-dimensional view which focuses on the exercise of power, rather than the potential to exercise power. It looks almost at the physicality of power, the end result of the relationship; that one individual has made another individual do something they would not have otherwise done.

Machiavelli discusses different types of Princes and principalities in his work. There are principalities that are won by money and foreign arms, power that is won by criminality and power of a principality that is constitutionally given. The latter is the most similar type to the political democracy we see today. Machiavelli claims that constitutional principalities are created by either one of two groups of people:

> A principality is created either by the people or by the nobles, according to whether the one or the other of these two classes is given the opportunity. A man who becomes prince with the help of the nobles finds it more difficult to maintain his position than one who does so with the help of the people. As prince, he finds himself surrounded by many who believe they are his equals, and because of that he cannot command or manage them the way he wants. A man who becomes prince by favour of the people finds himself standing alone, and he has near him either no one or very few not prepared to take orders. (Machiavelli, 1961: 30–31)

However, no matter whether the power and control is won by money, criminality or constitutional permission, power is a fixed, abstract sum. It is something to be taken or to win. It is not seen as two-dimensional (see Bachrach and Baratz 1970, later) and it is certainly not as developed as the fluid type of control discussed by Foucault (1980).

Marx discusses power in relation to 'money' and 'labour production'. These laws of money and capital were used, by capitalists, to control the workforce. The minutiae of their behaviour, both in and out of the work place, were controlled so that they could produce the 'surplus value' necessary to increase the capital owned by the capitalists. Marx famously predicts that with the increase in exploitation, there will also be an increase in working class revolt:

> Centralisation of the means of production and socialisation of labour at last reach a point where they become incompatible with

their capitalist integument. Thus integument is burst asunder. The knell of capitalist private property sounds. The expropriators are expropriated. (Marx, 1999: 379-80)

Marx's theories on power fit with the traditional zero-sum models of power. In his work Marx describes power (money, capital, labour production) as an entity which belongs to one group of people — the capitalists; and it must be wrested from them by another group of people — the workers. A Marxist approach to examining power relations in society has shaped researchers' views in understanding the categorisation and discrimination of certain groups in society.

Gramsci's *Prison Notebooks* look at a plethora of theorists, such as Marx and Machiavelli. The definition of power seems to be similar: zero-sum power that is either in the hands of one person/party/ group, or another. However, Gramsci starts to look at whether force is effective in this type of power:

> The problem is the following: can a rift between popular masses and ruling ideologies as serious as that which emerged after the war be 'cured' by the simple exercise of force, preventing the new ideologies from imposing themselves? (Gramsci, 1971: 276)

Gramsci's observations make points that are pertinent to the theme of this research — the identification, surveillance and control of 'anti-social' groups, namely Gypsies, by society. Gramsci talks about 'voluntarism and social masses'. He defines 'volunteers' as 'Gypsy bands and political nomads' (pg 275). On the control of 'volunteers' he says:

> ... no account is taken of the following factor: that the actions and organisations of 'volunteers' must be distinguished from the actions and organisations of homogenous social blocs, and judged by different criteria. (Obviously, 'volunteers' should be taken as meaning not the *elite* when this is an organic expression of the social mass, but rather those who have detached themselves from the mass by arbitrary individual initiative, and who often stand in opposition to that mass or are neutral with respect to it.) (Gramsci, 1971: 202-3)

Further on in his writing, Gramsci's view on these 'volunteers' — these Gypsy bands and political nomads — becomes a little confusing. In his point above he states that no account has been taken of the fact that there are 'volunteers' — those who detach themselves from society arbitrarily. Presumably, by saying this, he means that account should be taken of them now. However, later in his *Prison Notebooks* he says:

> Gypsy bands or political nomadism are not dangerous phenom-
> ena, and similarly Italian subversivism and internationalism
> were not dangerous. (Gramsci, 1971: 275)

Gramsci's ideas hold a resonance with the hypothesis that certain
groups — such as Gypsies and Travellers — are seen as 'other'.
Current and immediately previous governments in England have
certainly seen merit in distinguishing the actions of 'volunteers';
perhaps today these would incorporate the socially excluded — such
as Gypsies and Travellers. The government, with help from societal
discourse and the media, distinguish these actions so that the rest of
society — the 'homogenous social bloc' can keep a controlling eye on
them to prevent a disruption of current social order and power hierarchy.

Bachrach and Baratz (1970) define power:

> A power relationship exists when (a) there is a conflict over val-
> ues or course of action between A and B; (b) B complies with A's
> wishes; and (c) B does so because he is fearful that A will deprive
> him of a value or values which he regards more highly than those
> which would have been achieved by non-compliance. (Bachrach
> and Baratz, 1970: 24)

The two-dimensional type of control is not the zero-sum, traditional
power that Lukes refers to in his first classification, but nor is it as
fluid as the control and power relationships that Foucault discusses.
It is a middle-way of control. Power and control, according to
Bachrach and Baratz is not an abstract object, it is relational. The
intensity and usefulness of the control is entirely dependent upon
the recipients' perceptions. Lukes (1974) acknowledges Bachrach's
help in developing the three-dimensional view of power. However,
he does criticise the two-dimensional view (as exemplified by
Bachrach and Baratz) for not taking a wider sociological perspective
and for trying to define non-decision making as decision making
(Lukes, 1974: 50).

The focus of the two-dimensional view of power is the demonstra-
tion of power (either consciously or unconsciously) by the prevention of one person or group, by another, from stating contradictory
views which may be detrimental to the predominant cause or policy
of the day. An example of this might be where the majority of society
prevents any discourse around Gypsies and Travellers from contra-
dicting that which is widely held — e.g. that they are anti-social and
that they should conform to the norm of living in a house.

Foucault's Approach and the Three-Dimensional View

Lukes (1974) discussed the three-dimensional view in terms of having built upon the previous two views, in order to include a wider sociological perspective on power and to demonstrate its complexities and the difficulties of studying power. So that theoretical examples of these complexities and difficulties can be provided, it is necessary to turn to the work of Foucault. Foucault wrote prolifically on notions of power and control and he included many different elements of power. Foucault (1977 and 1980) examined techniques of power, particularly in relation to the prison and the hospital. Three main techniques were outlined. Firstly, discipline was examined as power, particularly in relation to disciplinary actions over the human body. This technique was really looking at physical force and as such it may relate to more traditional views of power and fit in the one-dimensional view. Secondly, training can be used as a form of control; this is exemplified not just in prisons but in the routines of schools and monasteries. Training is a more implicit form of control; it is focused on the inculcation of norms, which is problematic (the problem of social norms is examined in chapter seven). If a person refuses to conform to training they may be subject to discipline; in order to know whether there is conformity, a third technique of control is necessary — that of surveillance. These three techniques of control are discussed in various works by Foucault (1969, 1972, 1977, 1980) and are examined within different contexts. The latter two techniques, of training and surveillance, are more sophisticated and are more relevant to providing an example of Lukes' (1974) three-dimensional view. Training is discussed in terms of social norms in chapter seven, and surveillance is examined under Foucault's theory of the gaze, later in this chapter. Before moving on to an analysis of surveillance and the gaze, it is necessary to step back and look at the context for the exercise of power. One example of the exercise of power and control techniques is through discourse. Discourse is inextricably entwined with power in a large amount of Foucault's work and it is discussed in part, in this chapter. However, discourse is predominantly the domain of chapter five, where Foucault's theories are discussed alongside a number of other works.

Another context for the explanation of power and control is that of governmentality (Foucault, 1994). Governmentality, according to Foucault, is the 'art' of government. He talks about the changing emphases in government over history. Foucault (1994) refers to three main stages of government:

> First came the state of justice, born in a territoriality of feudal type
> and corresponding in large part to a society of law — customary
> laws and written laws … Second, the administrative state, born
> in the fifteenth and sixteenth centuries in a frontier and no longer
> feudal territoriality, an administrative state that corresponds to a
> society of regulations and disciplines. Finally, the state of
> government, which is no longer defined by its territoriality, by
> the surface it occupies, but by a mass: the mass of the population
> … And this state of government, which is grounded in its popu-
> lation and which refers and has resort to the instrumentality of
> economic knowledge, would correspond to a society controlled
> by apparatuses of security. (Foucault, 1994: 221)

Foucault's essay on governmentality was written up from a series of
lectures given in the late 1970's and he specifically referred to the
power of governmentality as having the population as its target of
power. However, this seems to contradict his work *Power/Knowledge*,
which was published in 1980, where he says that power does not
have a 'target' as such:

> Power is employed and exercised through a net-like organisa-
> tion. And not only do individuals circulate between its threads;
> they are always in the position of simultaneously undergoing
> and exercising this power. They are not only its inert or consent-
> ing target; they are always also the elements of its articulation. In
> other words, individuals are the vehicles of power, not its point
> of application. (Foucault, 1980: 98)

It is important to remember that the 'target' population is also a
'vehicle of power' according to the latter Foucaultian definition. The
fluidity of power, and the importance of perception and the relationships between individuals and between individual and government
is demonstrated in Foucault's definitions of power and governmentality (1980); this is not a uni-directional process of power and
government. The power of governmentality is a multi-directional,
relative concept. It is not a hierarchical, disciplinary, traditional
concept of power.

Danaher (2000) agrees with this summation of governmentality as
a multi-directional flow of power:

> That is to say, because governmentality is as much about what
> we do to ourselves as what is done to us, this opens up the possi-
> bility that we might intervene in this process of self-formation.
> (Danaher et al, 2000: 83)

Another important concept, that is inherent in the first explanation
of governmentality, is knowledge. The ensemble to which Foucault

refers does not just consist of institutions and procedures, but it also includes analyses, reflections, calculations and tactics. Modernity has allowed for increased knowledge by governments about what the population is doing; partly this is through surveillance of the population.

Society plays a more interactive role in governmentality, it does not have things done to it, but instead it responds to and changes the direction of power. However, modernity has allowed government more knowledge about the population. This knowledge does allow government additional control over different groups in society. As it knows more about the behaviour of individuals and groups, it can devise different methods of controlling this behaviour.

Views on government and society differ. An Enlightenment view is that of a social contract (Rousseau, 1994) where it is assumed that everyone has agreed to conform to some overarching norms of society and will abide by them, for the good of the whole. An opposing, more traditional, view of power sees different groups within society wresting power from other groups and then setting rules and laws that fall in with their values and hopes. Foucault's governmentality actually takes a middle ground between the social contract and the more traditional, zero-sum, views and sees that rather than power being grabbed and maintained by groups there is a rationality about the use of power. So instead of fighting over power as an abstraction there is instead thought about how power can be used most efficiently in society. (Danaher, 2000: 89)

Foucault's 'Gaze'

Foucault's 'gaze' might best be described as the eye of power and control. In *The Birth of the Clinic* Foucault describes gaze, thus:

> ... the gaze is not faithful to truth, nor subject to it, without asserting, at the same time, a supreme mastery: the gaze that sees is a gaze that dominates. (Foucault, 1969: 39)

The crucial element in the gaze is the interpretive element. Foucault (1969) was discussing it in relation to doctors looking at illnesses in their patients. He explained that doctors no longer passively viewed symptoms, but instead started to actively interpret them. This is important because my research attempts to link theories of the gaze with those of discourse and it raises the notion of discourse as control. The gaze is not passive surveillance, but active interpretation and domination. It is suggested that this is also true of discourse.

Words and terms used in the discourse around Gypsies and Travellers are not passively describing a situation but instead they are interpreting them. The interpretation involved in discourse is based on a variety of variables including the ontology of the speaker and their social norms and characteristics (this is discussed further in chapters five and seven).

Surveillance of different people in society can be rooted in different motives. Lyon (2002) sees that motives may have changed over ages:

> But what is all this 'watching' for? This too, is in flux. Once, police kept an eye on a specific person, suspected for some good reason of an offence. Or the debt collector tried to track down defaulters who owed money to others. While such practices still occur, much more likely is the creation of categories of interest and classes of conduct thought worthy of attention. If the modern world displayed an urge to classify, today this urge is endemic in surveillance systems ... to capture personal data triggered by human bodies and to use these abstractions to place people in new social classes of income, attributes, habits, preferences, or offences, in order to influence, manage, or control them. (Lyon, 2002: 3)

Surveillance studies—not just the internalised gaze, but overt surveillance—is a growing theoretical phenomenon—see Gandy (1993), Staples (2000), Schoeman (1992) and Lyon (2001 and 2003). A lot of this work is embedded in technological theory and the implications, for privacy, of the advances in information technology. However, all have their roots in the principles of Foucault's interpretation of Bentham's panopticon in order to understand what is meant by surveillance.

It is important to remember that the gaze is a metaphor, but it is a useful explanation of surveillance at work in society as a tool of control. McNay (1994) discusses this different perception of power and control:

> Control in modern societies is achieved, therefore, not through direct repression but through more invisible strategies of normalization. Individuals regulate themselves through a constant *introspective search for their hidden 'truth'*, held to lie in their innermost identity. (McNay, 1994: 97) [*Emphasis added*]

This introspective search for a hidden truth is part of the internalisation of the gaze, and it is discussed later in the chapter. McNay's quotation is useful to show how the gaze fits more with governmentality than traditional forms of government and power. The gaze does not use direct repression or other such authoritative power; it is not such a visible method of control as say sovereignty or discipline.

Foucault believed that the gaze was not only exemplified in the panopticon of Bentham's 18th-century prison designs, but could be extended, through institutions, to the wider society.

> ... the best way of managing prisoners was to make them the potential targets of the authority's gaze at every moment of the day. And this authoritative gaze didn't reside in a particular person, rather it was recognised as part of the system, a way of looking that could operate as a general principle of surveillance throughout the social body. This logic of the gaze, like that of discipline, was not confined to the prison, but moved throughout the various institutional spaces in society. (Danaher *et al.* 2000: 54)

Cohen (1985) criticises Foucault's lack of clarification (this is a common criticism of Foucault as there can be ambiguities across his large volume of works). Cohen explains panopticism:

> Surveillance and not just punishment became the object of the exercise. The all seeing world of Bentham's panopticon is the architectural vision of the new knowledge/power spiral: the inmate caught in a power which is visible (you can always see the observation tower) but unverifiable (you must never know when you are being looked upon at any one moment). The prison is the purest form of the panopticon principle and the only concrete way to realize it. (Cohen, 1985: 26)

This book does not fully concur with Cohen. I do agree that the prison is the purest form of the panopticon, but believe that there are other ways of realising it. Partly, this is through society's gaze — which is dominating through active interpretation rather than passively watching.

The prison serves as a useful example of the panopticon principle; but it can also help to understand the ideas of governance and the fluidity of power in society. For instance, in October 2002 there was a serious riot in Lincoln prison and it took over 400 police and prison officers to bring the prisoners back under control. On the Radio Four 'Today' programme there was an ensuing debate as to what had caused the riot. Professor Wilson, of the University of Central England, explained that 'the dirty little secret behind our prisons' was that they relied on prisoners' consent. The prisoners consented to be governed by the prison officers as long as their conditions were good and they were treated fairly. When there was a situation of overcrowding and prisoners were kept in their cells for more hours each day with fewer resources, they rebelled to show that they had withdrawn their consent to be governed (Wilson, 2002). This example in the prison is a good explanation for wider society. Consent to be governed is important (Rousseau, 1994) and those that withdraw it could be seen to be excluding themselves from a society which has an implicit consent to be governed in-built. Gypsies and Travellers are an example of a group who could be perceived to have withdrawn their consent to be governed—both by social norms and by legislation. The travelling lifestyle does not accord with the 'norm' of living in a permanent dwelling and the act of unauthorised camping is a rebuttal of the Criminal Justice and Public Order Act (1994).

Foucault did not just believe in the manifestation of the gaze in physical things, such as Bentham's panopticon, or a modern day example—surveillance cameras; he believed that the gaze was internalised. Through socialisation (for example, undergoing training or conforming to discipline on societal norms) individuals understand how they should behave, and they monitor themselves accordingly. Danaher *et al* (2000) recognise that there are different dimensions to the gaze—for instance a difference in the gender internalisation of the gaze. They discuss a well-used example of how women view media images of how women 'should' look—for example, magazine pictures showing the ideal woman being fit and thin. Amongst some women, there is a perceived duty to conform to this image and they follow beauty and slimming regimes in order to do this. These women have taken on the notion of how they should fit into society and they have internalised this and conformed; and through regular dedication to going to the gym and berating themselves for weight gain, they monitor themselves.

Although Danaher *et al* (2000) use different examples of the internalisation of the gaze, they do not help us to understand why the gaze is internalised by some people and not others, although there may be psychological studies which can help to explain this on an individual level. This comes back to the issue of different group and individual norms—why do some individuals believe in different norms to the rest of a group, or to other individuals? If internalisation of the gaze, as a tool of power, is dependent on everyone internalising the same, common values then there will never be internalisation wholesale of one value in society, because of different individual and group norms. For instance, the above example of women monitoring how they look in line with what society deems as 'normal'—some women will not agree with the norm being imposed upon them and will carry on living according to their own individual values—they will eat what they like, wear what they like and behave how they want. They will not internalise an imposed norm. Similarly, Gypsies and Travellers could be viewed as eschewing the norm of living a settled life in a house. However, this meta-norm of society, of house dwelling, does not accord with the long history of the norm of nomadism of the Gypsies and Travellers. In some current examples Gypsies are forced to accept the settled norm because there is no alternative accommodation provision, but others refuse to do this and will not give up their norms.

In order to shape behaviour, it is necessary to know how people are behaving and to have constraints, incentives and punishments in place to modify that behaviour, where it does not fit in with societal norms. The gaze as a technique of surveillance and of power is vital to this shaping of behaviour, vital to the art of government.

It has been seen in earlier discussions on the three dimensions of power that one of the ultimate forms of power is for B to assume the norms of A without knowing they are doing so. But is it possible for A to tell whether B has really assumed norms or whether they are pretending to in order to stop being put under overt, external, surveillance. Vaz and Bruno (2003) discuss Foucault's gaze and interpretation of the panopticon and they assume that the docility of B would only be a 'mask' carried as long as they felt that A was observing.

> To put it differently, we would internalize power's eye but we would not identify with its values. In reality, instead of an unfolding of ourselves in consciousness and its object, our conduct, we would experience a threefold partition of our interiority. We would distance ourselves from our behaviours and look at them with power's internalized eyes. However, there would be an additional detachment: a part of ourselves constituted by our consciousness and desire would be sheltered from power's eyes. (Vaz and Bruno, 2003: 276)

The idea of a hidden 'self' within a mask of internalised gaze strikes a chord with a section of the Gypsy/Traveller population. Some Gypsies and Travellers, there are no definitive figures to enable one to know how many exactly, have settled in permanent houses; occasionally this is through choice, because illness has stopped them from leading a nomadic lifestyle; or it is through 'coercion'. Gypsies and Travellers are coerced, by the state, to live in houses because there is no alternative provision for them; as discussed in chapter two, there are not enough Travellers' sites. In a variety of studies, including Niner (2003) where Gypsies and Travellers are asked their views, they say things such as 'travelling is in the blood'. Comments from Gypsies and Travellers describe the travelling lifestyle as beyond nomadism, and as such they still feel like Gypsies/Travellers even when they are in a settled house. This 'travelling in the blood' is an example of the hidden part of the self within the internalisation of the norm of living in a house. To all intents and purposes a Gypsy/Traveller living in a house has bowed to the generic societal norm of living a settled life—however, it is not an observable fact that they have really internalised this gaze, indeed anecdotal comments from Gypsies and Travellers point to the converse.

There is always someone who has the power to watch over us in various different aspects of our lives. Foucault says:

> A constant supervision of individuals by someone who exercised power over them—schoolteacher, foreman, physician, psychiatrist, prison warden—and who, so long as he exercised power, had the possibility of both supervising and constituting a knowledge concerning those he supervised. A knowledge that was no longer about determining whether or not something had occurred; rather, it was about whether an individual was behaving as he should, in accordance with the rule or not, and whether he was progressing or not. (Foucault, 1994: 59)

There are different ways of examining the 'gaze'. One way to start is by looking at explicit techniques and implicit techniques. For instance, an explicit technique of the gaze is the use of CCTV cameras in areas that suffer the consequences of 'anti-social' behaviour. An implicit technique, that has already been discussed, is the portrayal of a categorised group in the news media. Yet another implicit method is through television—soap operas and films can inculcate patterns of behaviour. Think of the discussion in the press of the 'suitability' of certain characters as 'role models for young people' or of the rows over whether violence on television instils unacceptable norms amongst the viewers. These media images are implicit ways of controlling and shaping behaviour—they are implicit mechanisms of the gaze.

Fopp (2002) looked at 'increasing the potential for gaze, surveillance and normalisation' by examining an Australian homelessness policy. He found that the homelessness policy under scrutiny kept families in short-stay, agency funded accommodation, for longer than they needed to. This was because of a lack of affordable long-term accommodation to go into. However, the outcome of the increased stay in the short-stay accommodation meant that the homeless families were under the watchful eye of the agency and they were therefore under a surveillance and normalisation regime.

Hier (2003) examines welfare monitoring to exemplify surveillance practices as processes of social control. He discusses the concept that increasingly different surveillance techniques are being brought together into an overall 'surveillant assemblage'.

> Although this characterizes an increasing pattern in surveillance, particularly where electronic or automated surveillance is concerned, it is important not to lose sight of the fact that these infrastructures remain connected to, or develop out of, 'early modern' systems of surveillance, underscored by the desire to coordinate and control populations, to make 'visible' that which evades immediate perception – the panoptic impulse. (Hier, 2003: 403)

The motivation of surveillance techniques to make visible that which evades perception – Gypsies and Travellers – is a focus of surveillance and control of which one should not lose sight. However, the efficiency of so-called 'surveillant assemblages' could be in dispute, in the light of high profile failures. In the early part of 2004 an investigation was underway into how the murderer Ian Huntley's previous alleged behaviour went undetected. Huntley was given a job as a caretaker in a school in Soham, Cambridgeshire and he was found guilty of the high profile murders of Holly Wells and Jessica Chapman. The police, in various counties, had kept records of alleged crimes committed by Huntley, but because of confusion over the implications of the Data Protection Act (1998), much of the information was deleted from electronic, shared, files. This case does not indicate a 'surveillant assemblage' but instead highlights the gaps in surveillance and record keeping across different agencies. However, it is just one high profile example of how surveillance measures can break down and it shows the failures of technology and those operating the technology.

It is necessary to highlight the importance of Foucault in the discipline of control and surveillance theories; this helps to explain my focus on Foucaultian theories to understand power and control. Wood (2003) sums up the perceived importance of Foucault to the discipline: 'When I was talking to colleagues about the theme of this issue, it was put to me that: "surely every issue of *Surveillance and Society* is a Foucault issue".' (Wood, 2003: 235)

Critique and Use of Foucault's Theories

Although widely used, Foucault's theories do not escape criticism. McNay (1994) asserts a Marxist critique of Foucault's explanations of power:

> Many of the problems that arise with Foucault's theory of power are related to the fact that a multiplicity of divergent phenomena are subsumed under a totalizing and essentially undifferentiated notion of power. In short, the concept of power is generalized to such an extent that it loses any analytic force. Many Marxists have accused Foucault of a lack of differentiation in his theory of power which results in a reductionist and functionalist account of processes of social control. There is a certain irony to these criticisms in so far as Foucault elaborated his theory of power in contradistinction to the economic reductionism that, in his view, hampered Marxist analysis. (McNay, 1994: 104-5)

Habermas (1987), one of Foucault's most vocal critics, also has problems with the 'undifferentiated' notions of power, as he feels that they do not reflect the complexities of modern society. Habermas does not agree with Foucault's rejection of modernity in his explanations. He also suggests problematic contrasts between social theory and systems of knowledge:

> ... discourses emerge and pop like glittering bubbles from a swamp of anonymous processes of subjugation. With his energetic reversal of the relationships of dependency among forms of knowledge and practices of power, Foucault opens up a problematic of social theory in contrast to the rigorously structuralist history of systems of knowledge ... (Habermas, 1987: 268-9)

Habermas also criticises Foucault's own approach to discourse analysis:

> Foucault wants to eliminate the hermeneutic problematic and thus the kind of self-relatedness that comes into play with an interpretative approach to the object domain. The genealogical historiographer should not proceed as does the practitioner of hermeneutics; he should not try to make comprehensible what actors are doing and thinking out of a context of tradition interwoven with the self-understanding of the actors. (Habermas, 1987: 276-7)

This particular criticism of Foucault links strongly with advice provided by Heuss (2000). The importance of context is vital in the 'practice of hermeneutics' particularly in relation to Gypsies and Travellers.

The critiques of Foucault's work are necessary here in order to demonstrate a thorough approach to the use of his theories of power and control. Not all theorists agree with Foucault's approach but these could be due to epistemological differences amongst research-ers. In spite of the critiques, Foucault's work continues to be used and developed in a number of studies, because it has much to offer those studying power and control, particularly in relation to dis-course.

Donzelot discusses, in his work *The Policing of Families* (1979), government through family. He examines the implications of the involvement of the family in the political:

> This direct insertion of the family into the political sphere of the *ancien regime* had two consequences for the exercise of social power. With regard to the central apparatuses, the head of the family was *accountable* for its members. In exchange for the protection and recognition of the state, he had to guarantee the faithfulness to public order of those who were part of that order; he also had to supply a fee in taxes, labor (corvees) and men (militia). Consequently, the fact of not belonging to a family, and hence the lack of a sociopolitical guarantor, posed a problem for public order. This was the category of people without ties, without hearth or home, of beggars and vagabonds who, being in no way connected to the social machinery, acted as disturbers in this system of protections and obligations. There was no one to supply their needs, but neither was there anyone to hold them within the bounds of order. (Donzelot, 1979: 49)

Although Donzelot, refers to an *ancien regime* several centuries ago, there is similarity with the expected function of the family in society today. For instance, as well as anti-social behaviour orders and curfews for youths who act in an anti-social manner — there are also parenting orders that penalise the parents of anti-social youths. This is quite an explicit contract between the government and the family.

Donzelot, also discusses three 'philanthropic poles' of power held over the family: moralisation, normalisation, and contract and tutelage. These three forms of power have commonalities with the three different types of power (discipline, training and surveillance) identified by Foucault (1977). Donzelot talks about the power of surveillance over the family to ensure that it meets the norms expected of it. He says:

> Leaning on one another for support, the state norm and philan-thropic moralization obliged the family to retain and supervise its children if it did not wish to become an object of surveillance and disciplinary measures in its own right. (Donzelot, 1979: 85)

This work by Donzelot reinforces the gaze and surveillance explanations of control by Foucault. Not only is the gaze internalised indi-
vidually, but there is an element — according to Donzelot — of the
family internalising the gaze as a unit, in order to deflect surveillance
techniques of the state and the wider neighbourhood.

This, brief, examination of Donzelot's policing of the family also
links well to some research by Gould (1988) which examined the
Övervakare in Sweden. The Övervakare were ordinary members of
the Swedish community, employed by the state as an explicit form of
social control over problem families. Where a child was thought to
be at risk of a neglectful, alcoholic or other troubled parent, the
Övervakare would keep a surveillant eye over the family and could
report to the state. Although the Övervakare could have been seen to
act in a mentoring role, there was no doubt that they were manifesta-
tions of the gaze in Swedish society and they were deployed in the
absence of what Donzelot referred to as the internalisation of the
gaze as a family unit. The Övervakare were provided for in law in
1902 and in some, less institutionalised, form have been used since.
However, Harloe (1995) in explaining the origins of the title of his
book stated that:

> ... *The People's Home* — appropriates a word — *folkhemmet* —
> frequently used to characterize the distinctive approach adopted
> by the Swedish Social Democratic Party to the building of what
> was seen for many years as the most developed form of welfare
> capitalist regime in the world. It was first used in 1928 by one of
> the key figures of Swedish Social Democracy ... *Folkhemmet* was
> a vision of society with social, economic and political citizenship
> for all. (Harloe, 1995: 1)

In one of the most revered states, for its universalistic social policies,
there was an undercurrent of surveillance and gaze through the use
of Övervakare to keep an eye on those who had not internalised the
norms of childcare.

This interventionist approach to controlling 'anti-social' groups in
society is not new to social theory and it can be related to all sorts of
groups including Gypsies and Travellers.

Flint and Rowlands (2003) similarly look at intervention and at
normalisation. As part of their examination of intervention and
governmentality, they discuss the 'branding' of housing consumption. They state that citizenship is framed by a moral identification
but also by an identification of consumption — in this instance the
consumption of housing (this is particularly interesting in relation to
Gypsies and Travellers as not only do they not consume the 'normal'

owner occupied tenure of housing, they do not 'consume' housing at all). Flint and Rowlands refer to Rose (1999):

> It is useful to apply this commercial concept of branding to acts of governance that seek to prescribe socially sanctioned acts of consumption, through what Rose terms 'grammars of living' in which subjects are directed to align their own conduct through behaving in correct ways (Rose, 1999). (Flint and Rowlands, 2003: 224)

Rose (1999) uses Foucault's writings on governmentality as a starting point for his work — however, he does make clear that he is not a Foucault scholar and that he does not intend to transplant Foucault's work into his own theorising on the subject of power and control. As with most of the writers and thinkers on the subject of relational power, it is difficult to be sure which relationships warrant examination. Rose tries to be specific:

> The investigations of government that interest me here are those which try to gain a purchase on the forces that traverse the multitudes of encounters where conduct is subject to government: prisons, clinics, schoolrooms and bedrooms, factories and offices, airports and military organizations, the marketplace and shopping mall, sexual relations and much more. (Rose, 1999: 5)

It seems that Rose is saying that these power relationships — governmentality — know no bounds and that in any organisation or relationship there is scope for discovery. Rose uses 'freedom as a pathway into the analysis of government'. This is of interest in this book as the hypothesis of my research moots the idea that freedom is not tolerated — but instead undergoes surveillance. For instance, the freedom of Gypsies to choose a travelling life is not celebrated by government or society — but instead is highlighted through discourse and media and is then put under surveillance and normalisation techniques of power.

Rose specifically discusses the issue of control:

> The free citizen was one who was able and willing to conduct his or her own conduct according to the norms of civility; the delinquent, the criminal, the insane person, with their specialized institutions of reformation, were the obverse of this individualization and subjectivization of citizenship. (Rose, 1999: 233)

It is possible to suggest that anyone who is free from explicit imposed surveillance, either by government or society, is someone who has agreed to be imposed by the 'gaze' both internal and external. For instance, a free person has been normalised through education

—both formal and worldly education. They have then 'opted-in' to society and said 'yes, I will conduct my own behaviour in accordance with what the government and the majority of society want of me'. Those that want to be truly free of 'normalisation', to live to different rules than society stipulates, are the very people who face the most rigorous surveillance and the harshest discipline.

Garland writes about power and control in the context of the criminal justice system and he, like many other authors on the subject of power, has been influenced by Foucault's work. Although Garland's writing focuses on the punishment of crime and the measures of power and control involved with that, there is still much relevance of his work here. The methods that are employed in the criminal justice system—discipline, surveillance and training—are also evident in society at large; for example, they are not just tools with which to punish criminals. They are tools with which the law abiding, but non-normalised Gypsies and Travellers, are made to conform or be punished.

Garland does acknowledge that there are wider boundaries of control in society:

> We have to bear in mind, therefore, that the field of crime control involves the social ordering activities of the authorities *and also* the activities of private actors and agencies as they go about their daily lives and ordinary routines. Too often our attention focuses on the state's institutions and neglects the informal social practices upon which state action depends. (Garland, 2001: 6)

This description of power and control in the criminal justice system also acknowledges the intricate relationship between different structures and individuals that make up a power relationship; of course when one part of a structure changes, this will have a knock-on affect on other parts, as Garland describes. This type of discussion relates well to the work of Foucault (1980), where shifts in the relationship between people and things means that individuals are at one and the same time both givers and recipients of power and control. Garland (1990) also writes specifically on the subject of surveillance and how the constant collection and audit of detailed information on people is replacing the overt, and sometimes violent, repression of people through sporadic displays of physical power and control.

Conclusion

An examination of theories of power and control has been undertaken in this chapter; this has largely centred on analysis of Foucault's ideas on 'governmentality' and 'gaze'. The discussion on governmentality demonstrated the notion of fluidity of power between structures and individuals. This is an important concept for the theoretical framework discussed in the previous chapter. The explanation of Foucault's 'gaze' provides useful concepts with which to explain how the actions of certain groups, for example Gypsies and Travellers, are monitored and it also provides theoretical links with discourse theories (these are examined in the following chapter).

Foucaultian explanations of the gaze demonstrate how surveillance in society works. It allows for discussion of surveillance as a tool of control, whether it is the overt type of surveillance or the covert, internalised, gaze. In the absence of internalising the gaze, a more overt type of control is used through heightened societal surveillance operationalised through and by discourse. The discourse element of the theoretical framework is discussed in the next two chapters.

Therefore, although a variety of theories of power and control have been discussed so far, by way of explanation, it is the notion of the gaze which is most useful in the developing framework. Foucault's notion is not just transplanted wholesale into the analysis. Instead the idea of the gaze and its links with social norms (see chapter seven) is used to try and understand the affect of discourse on Gypsies and Travellers. It is a useful theoretical tool, to add to discourse theory and analysis of social norms, to examine the notion that discourse can be used as a method of controlling Gypsies and Travellers.

Chapter Five

Theories of Discourse

Introduction

> Foucault ... point[s] out that what comes between ourselves and our experience is the grounds upon which we can act, speak and make sense of things. For Foucault, one of the most significant forces shaping our experiences is language. (Danaher *et al.* 2000: 31)

The previous chapter discussed explanations of power and control and it specifically focused on Foucault's governmentality and gaze. Foucault described governmentality as a new type of power, which superseded sovereignty and discipline, that was made up of a complex system of apparatuses and knowledge. The gaze was defined, in its simplest form, in terms of the panopticon principle; but difficulties surrounding the internalisation of the gaze, and the problems of researching the invisible, were identified. Discourse was previously highlighted as an implicit manifestation of the gaze. In this chapter, discourse is examined more closely, but the links with control are maintained.

Firstly, definitions of discourse and language are discussed in the context of theories of control and power. Different methods of discourse analysis are then examined, culminating in a summary that highlights some predominant studies.

Language/Discourse is Power

Discourse can be a problematic, ambiguous term. So, it is important, that in this chapter, the terms discourse and language are discussed before moving on to look at how they are used as a tool of power and control.

> Language is legislation, speech is its code. We do not see the power which is in speech because we forget that all speech is a classification, and that all classifications are oppressive ... (Barthes, 1977: 460)

Barthes succinctly describes language as power, in his lecture to the College de France. He also talks of discourse in the same way — indeed the terms are used interchangeably. Barthes explains that he does this, not because language and discourse are the same thing, but that they are inseparable.

> It is not only ... the words ... which are subject to a system of controlled freedom, since we cannot combine them arbitrarily; it is the whole stratum of discourse which is fixed by a network of rules, constraints, oppressions, repressions, massive and blurred at the rhetorical level. Language flows out into discourse; discourse flows back into language ... (Barthes, 1977: 470)

It is important to note Barthes' view on language and discourse, their differences and yet their dependence upon one another, in linking theories of discourse and theories of control.

Barthes' patron at the College de France was Foucault and so when Barthes talked of power, it was in reference to the all pervasive, relational power; not the more traditional, zero-sum type of power. Eco (1986) reinforces this view that Barthes is talking about relational power:

> In fact, Barthes is too subtle to ignore Foucault ...; therefore he knows that power is not 'one' and that, as it infiltrates a place where it is not felt at first, it is 'plural', legion, like demons. (Eco, 1986: 240)

The main premise of Foucault's work on discourse and language is that it is not reactive. Discourse does not just describe an action or thought; indeed, for Foucault, discourse is productive.

> Language is capable of building up zones of meaning that serve as a stock of knowledge that individuals use in everyday life and which can be transmitted from generation to generation. These systems of meaning or discourse represent or describe the nature of the world or reality and become taken for granted. They tend to be seen as having independent, objective reality, which is above the subjectivity of individuals. This is partly because they are transmitted from generation to generation through socialisation and so people perceive that they are the reality of the world into which they are born. (Clapham, 2002: 61)

Foucault's ideas on the power of discourse, are found particularly in the following works: *The Order of Things* (1966), *The Archaeology of Knowledge* (1972), *Discipline and Punish* (1977), *The History of Sexuality, Volume One, The Will to Knowledge* (1976) and *The History of Sexuality, Volume Three, The Care of the Self* (1984a). Foucault's thinking on power does change over time and throughout his publications, indeed it would be remarkable if Foucault's discourse were not open to historicisation, much as he would expect us to historicise other discourse. Fairclough (1992) discusses the changes in Foucault's work on discourse:

> In his earlier 'archaeological' work, the focus was on types of discourse ('discursive formations'...) as rules for constituting areas of knowledge. In his later 'genealogical studies, the emphasis shifted to relationships between knowledge and power. And in the work of Foucault's last years, the concern was 'ethics', 'how the individual is supposed to constitute himself as a moral subject of his own actions'... (Fairclough, 1992: 39)

Historicisation is not the only factor that may occur in Foucault's writing. Foucault's own discourse on power and discourse analysis can be opened up to scrutiny. Are there textual silences in Foucault's discourse on discourse? At this point, the reader could ask the same question of this work, is it possible that the discourse in this book is neither ideological, nor subjective? What control function might the discourse in this research have? This discussion is raised here, not to put doubt on the motive behind this work, but to highlight the issue that research into discourse analysis is still itself part of a wider discourse. This wider discourse could be part of a mechanism of control, and a tool of power.

Foucault's work on discourse and power is important. He specifically links discourse and surveillance, below:

> The examination that places individuals in a field of surveillance also situates them in a network of writing; it engages them in a whole mass of documents that capture and fix them. The procedures of examination were accompanied at the same time by a system of intense registration and of documentary accumulation. A 'power of writing' was constituted as an essential part in the mechanisms of discipline. (Foucault, 1977: 189)

It is helpful at this point to sum up and clarify what is meant by discourse and discourse analysis. King (2004) provides a definition:

> Discourse theory goes further than merely an analysis of language, and has been developed into a thorough critique of ideology, hegemony and power relations. 'Discourse' can here be seen as a catch-all term for the social practices articulated through language. (King, 2004: 3)

Jacobs (1999) clarifies the link between discourse theory and power:

... power conflicts are actualised through language and that specific discursive practices are the medium in which power is exercised and dominance maintained. (Jacobs, 1999: 204)

Finally, Hastings (1999b) says that:

Post–structuralism, and Foucault's corpus in particular, are central to understanding what is at stake in the notion of discourse, particularly in terms of how language practices are thought to interact with other social practices. The key post-structuralist insight is that language constitutes or produces the concepts and categories we use to make sense of the world. (Hastings, 1999b: 10)

Foucault (1999) also discusses the notion of gaining control over an issue in language as a precursor to gaining control over it in reality. He discusses the discourse of sex and says:

As if in order to gain mastery over it in reality, it had first been necessary to subjugate it at the level of language, control its free circulation in speech, expunge it from the things that were said, and extinguish the words that rendered it too visibly present. (Foucault, 1999: 514)

This subjugation of 'sex' in language, in order to control it in reality, is interesting for the hypothesis of discourse as control in relation to Gypsies and Travellers. With regard to sex, Foucault was arguing that its presence in language heightened its presence in reality. However, discourse conspired to hide sex in language through textual silence and therefore to hide it in reality. I would argue that the Gypsy/Traveller discourse, whilst it may hide the needs of Gypsies and Travellers, heightens the presence of their 'otherness' which makes it easier for them to be kept under the surveillant gaze of society and controlled.

Methods of Discourse Analysis

There is a plethora of different discourse research methods to choose from, depending on the type of research being undertaken. Discourse Analysis is a popular type of research but it has faced criticisms:

... discourse is something everybody is talking about but without knowing with any certainty just what it is: in vogue and vague. (Widdowson 1995: 158)

To avoid Widdowson's criticism of being 'in vogue and vague' it is important to clarify the different types of discourse analysis. Neuendorf (2002: 4-8) in explaining what content analysis does, reveals a number of different types of analyses:

Summary of Discourse Methods

- Rhetorical analysis (emphasis is on how the message is presented, not what the message says)

- Narrative analysis (focuses on characters as carriers of the narrative)

- Discourse analysis (popular method for analysing public communication)

- Structuralist or Semiotic Analysis (focuses on deep structures and latent meanings)

- Interpretative analysis (focuses on the formation of a theory following coding and analysis of messages)

- Conversation analysis (empirical approach to analysing transcribed conversations)

- Critical analysis (emphasises the importance of culture in the analysis of media messages)

- Normative analysis (provides a checklist with which to examine histories—e.g. where a statement is seen as ethnocentric, rather than universally 'true')

Figure 4: Summary of Discourse Methods

There are many texts that attempt to explain discourse analysis, or variants thereof. Some of the important works in the area of discourse analysis (and discourse analysis and disadvantage) include: Billig and Schegloff (1999) Fairclough (1992, 1995, 2001) Fowler (1991) Jarworski and Coupland (1999) Reisigl and Wodak (2001) Riggins (1997) Schegloff (1987, 1997, 2002) Ten Have (1999) Van Dijk (1993, 1999a, 1999b) Weber (1990) Widdowson (1995) Wodak and Meyer (2001). These works cover a broad range of discourse analysis. Jarworski and Coupland, for instance have edited a Discourse Reader, which includes a number of authors on different types of discourse analysis. Fairclough wrote numerous books, one of the most interesting was his work (1992) *Discourse and Social Change* where he looks at discourse as a social theory through examinations of constructing social relations of the self. Fairclough's approach in looking to embed the discourse analysis in something, so that it is not abstract, is useful. My research aimed to embed discourse analysis in text, for instance media articles, and then look at how that discourse is interpreted into controlling actions. This should avoid Widdowson's (1995) accusations of being 'in vogue and vague'.

Some theorists see Conversation Analysis and Critical Discourse Analysis (CDA) as two opposite sides of a coin. However, others, such as Schegloff (1998), examine CDA more carefully and they suggest that the two analyses are part of the same. Schegloff argues that CDA:

> ... would require a conversation analysis to be carried out first, 'otherwise the critical analysis will not 'bind' to the data, and risks ending up merely ideological'. (Schegloff quoted in Meyer, 2001: 17)

Content analysis is an empirical approach to discourse analysis. For instance, to see how high up the agenda Gypsies and Travellers were in a political debate, one could look through relevant texts and count the amount of times these two words were mentioned.

Critical Discourse Analysis (CDA) seems to be the most predominant method of discourse research in the social theory field. However, there is an element of sharing amongst the methods. CDA has context as a core element, it does not just count the occurrence of words, or analyse particular phrases, without looking at the context in which the language is used. However, CDA does need an anchor; it needs to examine particular texts as examples (Schegloff, 2001). Therefore, CDA may consist of a part content analysis, or conversation analysis, but it then examines the findings in a wider context. This is the approach taken in this book, and in a variety of studies examined, below.

Discourse and Exclusion

Several discourse studies look specifically at discourse and race, or discourse and exclusion. Van Dijk (1993) for example, discusses how racism is reproduced. He reviews discourse analysis on both a micro and macro scale for this, stating that:

> However, at a more global level of analysis we may also distinguish structural 'orders of discourse', that is, complex, societal, political, or cultural *systems* of text and talk. (Van Dijk, 1993: 122)

This message from Van Dijk, endorses the emphasis placed on the Foucaultian explanation of power, which was discussed earlier in relation to Lukes' three-dimensional view.

Reisigl and Wodak (2001) also looked at discourse and race. Specifically they analysed post-war anti-semitism in Austria. Part of the methodology of their research was to code discourse about Waldheim (former secretary of the UN who ran for Austrian presidency in 1986, but stories about his involvement in the war and his anti-semitic stance were uncovered by the press). The researchers triangulated their method by matching Austrian media discourse with other media, such as the US media, in order to establish a balanced approach. Reisigl and Wodak's research serves as a useful example of coding information in the media.

Riggins (1997) includes papers from a variety of authors on a number of subjects. One of the papers, pertinent to this book, was Helleiner and Szuchewycz (1997) *Discourses of Exclusion: The Irish Press and the Travelling People*. They raise an interesting point:

> In the case of Ireland, a focus on elite discourse is important because discrimination and antagonism toward Travellers is commonly attributed to an unenlightened public or, more specifically, to the working class. By contrast, our analysis aims to demonstrate how the powerful discourses of the press contribute to the creation of an ideological context that legitimates coercive state policies, everyday discriminatory practices, and ultimately violence against Travellers. (Helleiner and Szuchewycz, 1997: 112)

Helleiner and Szuchewycz's work is important as they found that discriminatory discourse is not just internalised in the 'working class' but by 'society' as a whole. Also, it does not just end with the discursive practice, but discourse continues on to sanction political and sometimes physical action against Gypsies and Travellers.

Helleiner and Szuchewycz incorporate issues of normality and 'otherness'. They examine a particular article from 1967, which was an editorial in the Connacht Tribune containing conflicting discourses (see examination of Stenson and Watt, 1999, later in the chapter). This article was urging sympathy towards Travellers whilst at the same time propagating negative images and stereotypes. However, with regard to 'otherness' the editorial said:

> ... the wretched families among the itinerants are not people who rejected the normal pattern of community life ... They were born and reared to the wretched life they lead ... They never had a chance to sample the normal pattern of living and to develop a human dignity. (*Connacht Tribune* editorial, 1967, in Helleiner and Szuchewycz, 1997: 115)

The main focus of the editorial was to pity the Travellers and their 'otherness'. Indeed Helleiner and Szuchewycz say that the editorial was written in *Itinerant Settlement Week in Galway City*. This settlement discourse had two outcomes, one of upsetting the 'settled community' and the other of marking the Travellers out as 'other'. Whilst the discourse may be slightly different in articles today, to the 1967 editorial, the assumptions and stereotypes would not be dissimilar. If anything, the focus may have moved away from one of sympathy to one of discrimination and racism. Settlement and pressure to settle are two of the methods by which Gypsy and Travellers' 'otherness' have been controlled; but even when settled they are still seen as 'other' to some extent.

Marston (2000) links ideology and discourse analysis, and he argues that positivist approaches to policy analysis have not helped to address the way in which language constructs identities. In his examination of public policy in Queensland he found a rise in the use of the customer metaphor, and he says:

> Metaphor and word meaning have direct relevance to the theme of policy legitimation and identity construction. (Marston, 2000: 355)

The metaphor of 'Gypsy' and 'Traveller' is a powerful tool in constructing the social identity of Gypsies and Travellers.

Marston (2002) hits on an important note in organising discourse analysis:

> During data collection I was conscious of the need to ensure a temporal dimension was included in the study, particularly since policy texts are, in one part at least, documents drawing on historical discourses. Historicizing discourse is an important dimension of Foucault's approach to discourse, knowledge and power. (Marston, 2002: 86)

Haworth and Manzi (1999) also examine discourse changing over time. They particularly look at the judgemental discourse which accompanies changes in local housing management practices. They say that:

> … social policy discourse in Britain is the willingness to introduce an explicitly moral dimension into analyses of problems, with the result that increasingly punitive strategies are adopted. For example, current debates on welfare reform focus attention upon concepts of 'dependency', 'individual responsibility' and the importance of the work ethic whilst proposing reduced state support, in the guise of increased choice, for those failing to conform to approved standards of behaviour. (Haworth and Manzi, 1999: 153)

This historicisation of discourse is an important aspect to the study of language around Gypsies and Travellers. It is possible to see that where language used about other Black and Minority Ethnic groups is no longer socially acceptable, it cannot be said to be true of Gypsies and Travellers specifically. In other words the BME discourse has moved on, and discriminatory discourse is less acceptable in general; yet Gypsy and Traveller discourse remains in a rut, where discriminatory terms are often used.

Marston (2002) also highlights how a moral discourse was used to frame a policy problem. He specifically speaks of the position of 'bad tenant' in the housing moral discourse and he refers to a contrast between 'us' and 'them' (pg 86). In his explanation of the 'bad tenant' position Marston says this is used (in the policy setting) to silence dissent. For example, to be positioned against a policy set to deal with 'bad tenants' demonstrates an alignment with the 'bad tenants'. This moral discourse of 'us' and 'them' can again be seen in the Gypsy and Traveller discourse in the media and in public speech. The discourse sets out to position Gypsies and Travellers as 'other' in order to distance the speaker or writer from negative characteristics associated with Gypsies and Travellers. This work by Marston, looking at the 'bad tenant', links in well with Cohen's work (1980) on folk devils and moral panics. Gypsies have been made folk devils, consistently from about the 16th century (Hawes and Perez, 1996).

Marston (2004) provides a further theoretical link between the fluidity of power and control, and discourse analysis. He says:

> Resistance is an important social and political process; it is a force that illustrates micro-rebellions against dominating discourses at the organisational and societal level. The attention to resistance and the conception of subject positions as a site of struggle helps us to focus on the way that power takes on a discursive form. There is a pressing need to understand the way social identities and the attendant ideologies of legitimacy and entitlement are constructed in welfare discourses and how these relate to social relations of power. (Marston, 2004: 7)

The notion of the fluidity of control and the resistance of discourse is an important concept to discuss here. The discussion in chapter four, on Foucault and the third-dimensional view of power, made clear that control is not a simple action of A making B do something. It is much more subtle than that, and is dependent on perceptions and relationships between actors. This book however, looks at the notion that discourse is a tool of control, and it results in discriminatory actions over Gypsies and Travellers. Marston (2004) provides an important reminder of the complexity of relationships in discourse.

Although I moot the notion of what may be seen as quite a simplistic relationship between discourse and control over Gypsies and Travellers, there is evidence of resistance to dominant discourses, as suggested by Marston (2004). In the next chapter, there is a brief discussion on the newly formed Gypsy Traveller Media Advisory Group (GTMAG), which was set up specifically to resist dominant discourse. The GTMAG is a new group and it has only recently started to provide a vehicle for such a resistance. As such, it is suggested that the discourse and control over Gypsies and Travellers currently demonstrates a more simplistic dominance of society over the travelling minority. However, it will be interesting to see whether organisations such as GTMAG help Gypsies and Travellers to resist the dominant discourse in the future.

Discourse Analysis and Gypsies & Travellers

During the literature review on discourse analysis and on Gypsies and Travellers, there was a dearth of information on research which looked at applying discourse analysis to the issues of Gypsies and Travellers. Holloway (2002) examines this, but she applies the analysis of discourse to the writings about Gypsies in the late nineteenth and early twentieth centuries. She refers to a 'fluidity of otherness' in the discursive construction of the Gypsy:

> First, it shows that the meaning of the category Gypsy/gipsy was far from stable in the late 19th century and early 20th century. For example, taking national-level debates … highlighted the contemporaneous but contradictory meaning attributed to Gypsies by the romantic and reformist movements: whereas romantic writers and gypsiologists elevated Gypsies to the status of noble savages living in harmony with nature, reformists were more likely to label them as a deviant and criminal minority. (Holloway, 2002: 711)

This is still true today and the conflict of 'true/real' Gypsy as the good romanticised notion, versus 'fake' Gypsy/Traveller demonised as folk-devil is still relevant in contemporary discourse, both in the media and elsewhere.

Turner (2000) looks at discourse and Gypsies and Travellers and he examines more contemporary political discourse as well as analysing a small selection of press articles. He quotes Jack Straw:

Jack Straw believes that many Travellers 'go burgling, thieving, breaking into vehicles, causing all kinds of trouble, including defecating in the doorways of firms'. They are 'masquerading as law-abiding Gypsies, when many are not'. (Turner, 2000: 68)

Turner draws comparisons with other ethnic groups, particularly 'migrants'. Again, the issue of 'true' and 'fake' Gypsy becomes apparent. Straw seemed to think that he could tell who a 'real' Gypsy was and that he established that most Gypsies were not 'real' but instead 'masquerading'. Turner also, briefly, examined the press for examples of discriminatory discourse and found a variety of articles which reflected a negative image of Gypsies and Travellers. Finally, he looks at the issue of 'conformity versus identity' and says:

Paradoxically, Travellers who move into houses — where integration into settled society seems most complete — are the most isolated of all. Isolated in the environment they are in, because they are different and seen to be different, isolated because they are not with their family and kin. (Turner, 2000: 76)

This is reflected in a variety of ways, for example Niner's (2003) research includes statements from Gypsies and Travellers which resonate with this sentiment. It is also reflected in the discussion on the gaze in chapter four. Although the gaze, from an outsider's perspective, seems to have been internalised by the settled Traveller, there is still a secret part of themselves which has not internalised the 'gaze' and will remain independent from settled norms.

Turner (2002) examines the portrayal of Gypsies and Travellers by discourse in the Houses of Parliament, particularly the House of Commons. He states that the language used in Parliament is indicative of the esteem in which a particular group is held by politicians and policy makers. Turner refers to a parliamentary debate on 'the problem of Gypsies' raised by Ann Widdecombe. The discussion on Gypsies had followed on from a speech about dangerous dogs.

'Even where they are not directly responsible for assaults on the population, the behaviour of itinerants is a problem. Dogs and cats regularly disappear from nearby areas to these encampments'. Widdecombe's comments paid heed to the existence of a social hierarchy, even within the dog world: 'My distinguished predecessor, Sir John Wells, lost a pair of much-loved and valuable dogs'. The police were not interested; the local authority was not interested. Luckily, an "alert constituent", walking past an encampment, 'noticed two dogs that were cleaner and fitter not only than the other dogs but the occupants'.

Even extracted from the substantive points raised in the debate, the terms used are significant. Both dangerous dogs and Gypsies need 'control'; both are 'problems'.

Miss Widdecombe was very explicit about the need for 'control'. It was mentioned by her several times. Indeed, the British way of life itself was threatened. She closed her speech by arguing that there was a need to find a means of 'controlling the menace before it becomes a greater one, when it will no longer be so easy to bring it within the laws that apply to the rest of civilised Britain'.

(Turner, 2002: 7-8)

Turner discusses the language used by Widdecombe in the context of a discussion on Gypsies and Travellers as 'criminal by nature'. Turner's (2002) paper is particularly useful to this research in identifying themes in political discourse. These themes are summarised in figure five, below, as a reference point for the examination of discursive trends outlined later in the book.

Political Discourse Themes

- Criminal by nature
- Outside the community
- Menace
- Dirty
- Dishonest
- Immoral and amoral
- Nomadic
- 'real' and 'fake'

Figure 5: Themes outlined by Turner 2002

Erjavec (2001) demonstrates how discriminatory discourse is 'normalised' in the Slovenian media:

The syntactic structure of discriminatory discourse offered the readers categories which differed very little: the headline and the lead constructed a closed interpretation of the situation and the rest of the news report strengthened, legitimated and naturalized this interpretation especially with its use of evaluation. In order to create a coherent meaning of the news text, journalists first reduced the definition of the situation to only one event, which presented the majority population in a positive light. To construct only one, natural dominant interpretation of the ethnic discrimination they selectively (mis)used information, used discourse of difference with colonization of common-sense language, and the strategies of denial of discriminatory discourse. The majority population was the dominant group, responsible for the process of doing and saying as actors and sayers. The study of the Slovenia media adheres to the analytic paradigm of critical discourse analysis (CDA) (Erjavec, 2001: 699)

Erjavec found that Gypsies are not newsworthy unless they fit into a media stereotype. The problem occurs when they are reported as fitting into a stereotype — that stereotype is further reinforced and the discriminatory discourse becomes 'objective truth', because it is so well embedded in the public conscience. Erjavec looked at one specific incident in the village of Maline, Slovenia. She said that from September to October 1997 the villagers and the local authority prevented a Romani family from moving into a house they had legally bought and they then forced the family to sell the house. There was no public outcry to this act of discrimination and Erjavec felt that this was because of the way the discriminatory behaviour had been reported in the media. Erjavec examined 37 print media articles related to the incident and she looked in detail at how the news was reported:

> The villagers are depicted as the dominant actor in all the leads analysed. They are associated with the positive predicates of the material processes, such as guarding, defending, protecting. This gave the impression that the house is the property of the villagers and that they are making sure it is not appropriated. The construction of this meaning was effective because the journalist withheld a key piece of information, namely, that the Romani family had legally bought the house and that the villagers are violating the rights of the Roma to their property by preventing them from entering the house. The first sentence of the lead itself partially defines the situation as an event in which the villagers are guarding the house and, with selective (mis)use of the information, orients the reader to process the news report in a pre-determined direction. (Erjavec, 2001: 709-710)

This construction of news as 'truth' demonstrates the power of discourse in controlling Gypsies and Travellers, by putting the dominant group in the proactive, protecting, role and by leaving out vital information on the legality of the ownership of the Romany family's house. The reader of the article firstly does not know the truth of the situation, and secondly becomes complicit in the normalisation of discriminatory discourse.

Leudar and Nekvapil (2000) also looked at the representation of Romanies, but this time in Czech television debates. They examined conversations in debates between Czechs and Romanies and found that many descriptions were used and they were warranted as common sense, or universal truths. However, they found that the Romanies did not recognise the descriptions used by the Czechs, as they left out a lot of the positive, individualistic, characteristics of Romany Gypsies. They quoted sixteen examples of descriptions, from Czechs and Romanies, across four debates. It is worth including all sixteen examples here:

1. Romanies have a different mentality than white people, they express themselves differently, they look different.
2. They do not behave themselves like normal people.
3. They create hassles everywhere.
4. Gypsies have a distaste for work.
5. Gypsies should live like we do, following the laws, the rules of the game.
6. What interests them is money, sex and enough food.
7. They take as much as possible from the other.
8. The Gypsy ethnic group accounts for seventy, eighty per cent of criminality, and therefore they are an immense burden for this uh for this country.
9. Fifty to sixty percent of those criminal acts are really committed by the members of this ethnic group
10. The Romany ethnic group accounts for a considerable share of crimes like pick-pocketing or pimping.
11. Romanies simply commit a certain part of banal criminality.
12. People only knew about us that we steal, rob, murder.
13. Romany in the media equals thief, thug, jail bird, simply criminal element.
14. One pimps, steals, makes living pick-pocketing but the majority of Romanies are trying to look for work.
15. What is commonly said about us—incompetent, no know-how, they can't read, they do not have the intelligence.
16. Most Romanies are religious.

(Leudar and Nekvapil, 2000: 488-489)

The majority of these sixteen statements are negative and discriminatory, even those which have been made by the Romanies are defending against negative statements, rather than promoting positive statements. In my research for this book I found that there is more of a negative characterisation around mess and cost, whereas in the Czech media Leudar and Nekvapil show more of a focus on crime.

Clark and Campbell (2000) examine 'most' of the leading British daily and Sunday papers in the last two weeks of October, 1997; this was a time where the media and the public perceived there to be a Gypsy 'invasion' at Dover. They openly state that this was a 'selective investigation' and it aimed to examine the treatment, in the British press, of Czech and Slovak Romani Gypsies seeking asylum. They say:

> Alongside blatant ignorance and ideologically loaded commentaries, was the fact that the Roma were seen as 'soft targets' by staff writers and editors of the major newspapers. They were, in the words of one features writer ... 'fair game' and a group that could help 'sell copy'; their perceived 'exotic otherness' combined with their 'scrounging refugee' label gave newspaper columnists and editors a license to wax lyrical. (Clark and Campbell, 2000: 41)

Conclusion

Control in discourse, as a precursor to control in reality, is key to the hypothesis of this book. The control of Gypsies and Travellers can be demonstrated in a range of discourse — media, political, legislative and public; and this is discussed later. However, the real control over Gypsies and Travellers is in the translation of discourse into action. Examples of discourse into action have been discussed in the introductory chapter where Lodge (2004) discusses his treatment by the police. It is also examined later on, where legislation and policy discourse, and its interpretation, are analysed.

In chapter four, it was concluded that Foucault's notions on the gaze were of importance, amongst the theories of control, in developing a theoretical framework to discuss the findings of this research. Again, Foucault's theory of the links between discourse and control, discussed in this chapter, is an important component of the theoretical framework.

I have examined discourse as both theory and method, and the current research can be seen to fit almost entirely into the field of critical discourse analysis, as summarised below:

Critical Discourse Analysis	Research Examples	Gypsy/Traveller Examples
Description of Method *Interested in relationship between language and power. Links to language as social construction, looks beyond the language to its context.*	Foucault (1966, 1972, 1976, 1977, 1984a,b) Fairclough (1992, 1995, 2001) Wodak and Meyer (2001) Van Dijk (1993, 1999a, 1999b) Widdowson (1995) Billig (1999) Fowler (1991) Jarworski and Coupland (1999) Riggins (1997) Marston (2000, 2002) Haworth and Manzi (1999) Reisigl and Wodak (2001) Schegloff and Meyer (2001)	Helleiner and Szuchwycz (1997) Turner (2000 & 2002) Holloway (2002) Erjavec (2001) Leudar and Nekvapil (2000) Clark and Campbell (2000)

Figure 6: Examples of discourse research

A variety of research, including specific works on Gypsies and Travellers, was examined in this chapter and especially in the latter area there were common findings of discriminatory discourse. It is important that such empirical work is used to build up a picture of the discourse surrounding Gypsies and Travellers and that the primary research from this study is not analysed in isolation from the literature review in this area. Where this book takes one step further than the existing work is in mooting the notion that discourse is not just a reflection of people's views on Gypsies and Travellers; but indeed that the discourse can be 'operationalised' into actual control.

Chapter Six

Media Discourse

Talking about Gypsies and Travellers

Introduction

The biggest area of my primary research was an analysis of media articles, from all national and local newspapers, for one month in 2003. As such, the majority of discursive themes I found around Gypsies and Travellers were from media reports. These themes are included throughout this chapter, with a few (such as folk devils) being included in chapter seven. However, media discourse cannot be separated totally from public discourse and the discourse of Gypsies and Travellers, and this is included in the analysis of the themes.

The aim of this chapter is to outline the importance of media discourse to the debate on control, and to examine relevant literature on this subject. Examples of media articles will be examined and key themes brought out.

Discourse in the News

Fowler (1991) specifically looks at discourse in the news. He refers to news as practice:

> Thus news is a *practice*: a discourse which, far from neutrally reflecting social reality and empirical facts, intervenes in what Berger and Luckman call 'the social construction of reality'. (Fowler, 1991: 2)

This linguistic construction of social reality is a powerful tool in creating categories and sorting them into 'conflictual opposites' (Fowler, 1991: 6). With the example of Gypsies and Travellers, the news constructs Gypsies and the settled community as conflictual opposites. After a while this construction of reality sees Gypsies as embodying the enemy of the 'normal' settled community.

Fowler goes on to look at values in the news and he refers (pages 13-14) to a list of contextual factors formulated by Galtung and Ruge (1973). There are twelve factors in the list of news values. The concept for Galtung and Ruge, is that the more values there are in an event, the more newsworthy it is. For the purposes of this discussion though, the factor 'reference to persons' is important. Fowler analyses this:

> F11, 'reference to persons', or 'personalization', is also a socially constructed value. Its application varies a good deal from paper to paper (thus underlining its artificiality), being most striking in the popular Press. Presumably its functions are to promote straightforward feelings of identification, empathy or disapproval; to effect a metonymic simplification of complex historical and institutional processes (Arthur Scargill 'stands for' a whole set of alleged negative values in trades unionism; WPC Yvonne Fletcher, shot dead from a window of the Libyan Embassy while policing a demonstration, is made to stand for 'Britain's moral superiority over Libya') ... (Fowler, 1991: 15)

There is a possible extension to Fowler's analysis of Factor F11, in order to understand the treatment of Gypsies and Travellers in the press. What do Gypsies and Travellers 'stand for'? My findings from the media analysis on Gypsies and Travellers sees them as 'standing for' a cost to the taxpayer, causing a mess and being 'other' to the settled community. This case of the Gypsies and Travellers as standing for 'otherness', links again with the tool of control through Bauman's theory of proximity (1989), which is discussed in the next chapter. Fowler also discusses this in his analysis of Galtung and Ruge's Factor 4:

> F4 'meaningfulness'. 'Meaningfulness' with its subsections 'cultural proximity' and 'relevance', is founded on an ideology of ethnocentrism, or what I prefer to call, more inclusively, homocentrism: a preoccupation with countries, societies and individuals perceived to be like oneself; with defining 'groups' felt to be unlike oneself, alien, threatening. Presupposed is what several media specialists have helpfully identified as a consensual model of society. This is the theory that a society shares all its interests in common, without division or variation ... But although consensus sounds like a liberal, humane and generous theory of social action and attitudes, in practice it breeds divisive and alienating attitudes, a dichotomous version of 'us' and 'them'. (Fowler, 1991: 16).

This theory of consensus and consensual norms is discussed in detail in chapter seven, where there is an examination of Elster's (1989) theories on social norms. The other link between Fowler's analysis of media reporting and social norms, is with Cohen's work on the 'folk devil'.

Finally, though, Fowler emphasises the ramifications of stereo-typing in the press, it is not just a one-off occurrence but '... is in fact a reciprocal, dialectical process in which stereotypes are the currency of negotiation' (Fowler, 1991: 17). In other words, when an event is reported in the news it reinforces the stereotype; and the fact that a stereotype is part of the event makes it more newsworthy.

The media is not merely a reporting mechanism that reflects events and feelings, it helps instead to create and shape events and feelings. The media is now more pervasive than ever thanks to the improvement of information and communications technology. The news is shown on dedicated channels 24 hours a day and is updated in real time. The internet allows for email and websites that contain a variety of different news and views—all of which is accessible in many homes, offices, schools and libraries across the country. This accessibility of the media (and the accessibility of the population for the media to broadcast to) is a reasonably new phenomenon. It is for this reason, and in the current context of highly capable information and communications technology, that the media influence over public perceptions and actions should not be underestimated.

> As the confines of the prison, the convent, the family house, the neighbourhood, the executive suite, the university campus and the oval office are all invaded through electronics, we must expect a fundamental shift in our perceptions of society, our authorities and ourselves. (Meyrowitz, 1987: viii)

If one couples this pervasive nature of the media with the fact that 'news' is not published as hard data without a hint of bias, it is possible to see how a group not liked by the media can be its victim. It has been argued that the media picks up on the 'public mood' and reflects that in its reporting style in order to ensure its popularity and commercial viability. Steyn (1998) refers to the news as soap opera:

> For most people, news is something that crops up between sit-coms, soap operas and commercials, and it is not surprising that, over the years, it should have absorbed the same techniques as its colleagues. Most news anchors are, in essence, actors playing newsmen; their sets are fake newsrooms (BBC television's is computer-generated — in other words, even the set is an act of deception); increasingly, special reports are underlaid, like any

drama, with incidental, emotionally manipulative music, and from time to time, if the story lacks exciting visuals, it's easiest just to borrow from Hollywood directly: a recent NBC *Nightly News* story on the changing role of the CIA used clips from *The Spy Who Came in From the Cold*. (Steyn, 1998: 168-9)

Steyn is writing about media portrayal of news in the context of criticising it for being 'sentimentalized'. For the purposes of this chapter, it is a useful quotation to demonstrate how 'the news' is not immune to skew or bias, and how it is not just a reporting mechanism. It depends on the distribution channel for the news and who is 'telling' the news as to how distorted the facts might be. This means that the interests of those telling or producing the news will be reflected in the way it is told. Printed news stories about Gypsies tend to show bias against them. Also there is a tendency to distinguish between 'proper Gypsies', the traditional Roma, and New Travellers. Travellers are depicted as thieves and expensive to clear up after — with little regard for the facts of the matter.

There is a wealth of research in the field of media studies such as the work of the Glasgow Media Action Group. The Group's first publication (1976) was entitled *Bad News* and it focused on electronic media, in this instance television news. In its theoretical stance it is linked with the work from Fowler (1991) in its use of Galtung and Ruge's (1973) 'news values'. The values are classed as one of four main filtering processes for news; the other three being (1) time/resources, (2) 'television values' or what looks good visually, and (3) 'cultural air/ideological atmosphere' (Glasgow Media Action Group, 1976: x). Fowler (1991) is not a media analyst but uses some media studies theory in his discourse analysis of news media. The Glasgow Media Action Group are media analysts and their work overlaps with Fowler's at the point where discourse in the printed press is used as a comparison with the electronic media.

Talking about Gypsies

The portrayal of Gypsies in the popular press varies. However, the majority of features and reports do seem to rely on predictable, negative images. One article in the Evening Standard (2000) featured an article *Digging in against travellers*:

> Green fields and commons in Twickenham, Hampton Court, Barnet, Reigate, Walton on the Hill and Epsom have seen travellers pitch up before being driven off by legal action, only to leave behind piles of rubbish to be removed at council taxpayers' expense.

Local authorities say they are fighting a war of attrition, handicapped by a laborious legal process. It's a guerrilla campaign that has seen the travellers moved on from one site to another, taking advantage of open gates and legal delays to set up temporary home. (Sawer 2000: 11)

The core of this article seemed to be reporting on the fact that legal delays on eviction processes meant that Gypsies were illegally camping on London's common land. However, from the quotation above it would not be unrealistic to think the article was a call to arms against Gypsies. The first paragraph is telling Evening Standard readers that 'you, personally, are paying for rubbish clearance from Gypsy sites through council tax'. The second paragraph talks of a 'war' and a 'Guerilla campaign'. This is quite extreme wording for a feature reporting on Gypsy sites, and it could be seen to incite racial hatred toward Gypsies through its aggressive wording. This article is not a lone example of the media discourse on Gypsies and Travellers. In order to understand key discursive themes, I examined a number of newspaper articles which mentioned Gypsies and Travellers, and many of these were negative in tone; like the Evening Standard article, quoted above.

Media Analysis

The methodology of my research was previously outlined in Fig. 1, Chapter One. The articles I analysed in 2003 were largely negative in their tone to Gypsies and Travellers. Some, however, were positive in that they damned discrimination against Gypsies and Travellers.

Police are investigating claims of racism in an East Sussex village after residents attending a bonfire party burned a caravan with pictures of Gypsies painted on it. The vehicle, bearing the number plate P1KEY, was set on fire during Guy Fawkes celebrations in Firle, which was at the centre of a dispute over travellers earlier this year.

Local MP Norman Baker said residents were upset after 'itinerant criminals' caused damage to land and property, and a degree of anger was understandable. He backed the organisers of Firle Bonfire Society, who denied any racism, and pointed out that other figures such as the local police chief, President George Bush and Osama bin Laden had been given the same treatment at previous Guy Fawkes' celebrations. They claimed they were following a bonfire night tradition of burning effigies of things that had troubled the local community over the past 12 months.

But several parents who attended the event with children expressed concern at the tone of the event last Saturday, and the

Commission for Racial Equality has called for those involved to be punished. The CRE chairman, Trevor Phillips, said the burning was a clear example of incitement to racial hatred, a crime which carries a maximum sentence of seven years. 'You couldn't get more provocative than this,' he said. (Ellinor, 2003: 7)

The Firle bonfire article is an example of conflicting discourse about Gypsies and Travellers, both positive and negative. Despite it containing negative comments from the local MP, the general theme of the article is positive in that it seems to be damning the bonfire. An example of conflicting discourse was examined by Helleiner and Szuchewycz in their analysis of a Connacht Tribune article of 1967. The situation in Firle demonstrated an extreme form of prejudice against Gypsies and Travellers. Commission for Racial Equality (CRE) Chairman, Trevor Phillips, in the above article, noted how provocative the actions of the Firle bonfire party were. Indeed in another article in the Western Daily Press, Phillips said that the 'UK for Gypsies is still like the US Deep South for black people in the 1950's' (Western Daily Press, 2003a: 6). Certainly the burning of effigies is reminiscent of Ku Klux Klan activity in Southern America at that time.

Condemnation of the Firle bonfire did not stop with the CRE; a West Gypsy Rights spokeswoman, Maggie Smith-Bendall was quoted as saying:

> There is still an enormous amount of prejudice. In fact, we are treated like the Red Indians of America. *People want us to keep to reservations.* There has always been an inbred fear of the Romany. If Romanies move into a village and people find out, many will start saying that the gypsies will be stealing diesel and so on. When I put in for planning permission in the same village where my parents had lived for 30 years, I faced a huge amount of prejudice and people collected money to try to buy me out. (*Western Daily Press*, 2003a: 6) [*Emphasis added*]

Of the 'positive' reports on Gypsies and Travellers in October 2003, most were regarding the Firle bonfire party. Two articles looked at the traditions of the Stow Gypsy fair and wrote in a romantic style about the craft stalls and the horse trading. One article reported that Trevor Phillips wanted to see Gypsy/Traveller representation on the CRE board; and another report detailed the support that a local authority had given to Travellers, to stay on a site. The final report was written by a Traveller for a local paper. It was an open letter inviting local residents to visit the site and to meet the Travellers, to gather a true picture of their way of life. This letter also refuted some allegations made about the site. The Traveller wrote:

> 1. We did not force any padlock or gate to enter the site; we merely lifted off the chain and opened the gate which is left unlocked ...
>
> 2. We do not drive untaxed vehicles
>
> 3. We have not caused any damage to the land (or gate) and intend only to enhance the site
>
> *(The Cornishman, 2003b: 35)*

The Traveller defends some of the issues which are themes that come out of the analysis of the October 2003 reports, and more widely across all media reports and public debate that have been used in this research. The Traveller goes on to defend another assumption about Travellers' sites:

> This is not rural pastureland but a 'brownfield site' — and a highways dump and local fly-tipping spot which has been cleaned up, cared for and enhanced by a community of people who have appreciated living here and becoming part of the community and have felt, on the whole, very welcome. *(The Cornishman, 2003b: 35)*

The positive articles draw heavily on comments from 'insiders', for instance Gypsies/Travellers themselves or representatives from the Commission for Racial Equality. Positive comments are to be expected from these groups of people. However, in some instances there were also comments from local residents at the bonfire party, who were not connected to the travelling community, but who condemned the actions at Firle.

The majority of articles I examined were negative, and it was possible to categorise them according to broad themes, which have been outlined already. However, there was a mixture of articles that did not fit into any one particular category, but they still had a negative focus. A couple of articles discussed unauthorised encampments in the locality but they did not discuss mess or cost; some of the terms included 'ride roughshod' when the planning system was discussed. The articles presumed that Gypsies and Travellers got a better deal than the settled community. Another article looked at a hedge that had been 'destroyed' as a result of a caravan moving into a field. A further article was in a national paper (The Daily Mail) and it was analysing the work of Lady Brittan the Lottery Chief Executive. The title was *Axed, Queen of the Loony Lotto Grants*, and one of the grants it focused on was £190,000 to the Rural Media Company for a 'magazine about gipsy and traveller issues' (this is referring to *Travellers' Times* which is an important publication for the Travelling community) (Doughty, 2003: 15). Another article was in reference to a murder trial, where it was alleged that one Gypsy had murdered his relative. There was not a significant number of negative terms but there was a reliance on the fact that the case involved Gypsies when this was not the focus of the story; the murder should have been the focus. One final example of these 'general' articles was about damage to a bridge in Middlesbrough. It did not discuss cost or mess but instead referred to a piece of architectural heritage being destroyed. These articles could not each be coded, otherwise there would have been too many categories.

Cost and Mess

The theme of the 'cost' of Travellers stretches across the media and is not just limited to print. In a bulletin of East Midlands Today on BBC1 news, a reporter said:

> Money that was ear-marked for this year's Newark and Nottinghamshire show has already been spent on keeping Travellers off the site. Nearly £16,000 has been spent on security measures at the showground. On two occasions nearly 700 Travellers with 200 caravans have been removed from the site. (*East Midlands Today*, 2003)

One of the most significant themes to come out in the findings of the media coding and analysis, was that of cost and mess. There is an assumption that Travellers settle on green fields and then leave a mess. It is further suggested that any rubbish left on a Travellers' site was left there by Travellers; however, this is not always the case. One anecdotal example, from the Midlands, was where a caravan had pulled up on an unauthorised site — a patch of grass next to a lay-by. During the second night that the caravan was there a huge amount of trade rubbish was dumped next to the lay-by. The local press printed a number of stories blaming the Traveller for the rubbish. The local Gypsy Liaison Officer looked into the problem and found paperwork in the rubbish that included invoices addressed to a local builder, who had tipped the rubbish there. The local press did not print a correction to say that it had not been the Traveller; and the scrutiny that he faced, following the press articles, forced him to move on.

This anecdotal account is backed up by other research. A report by the Institute of Public Policy Research said that '… this actual and perceived link between Traveller and Gypsy communities and illegal waste dumping activities both gives rise to and exacerbates prejudice and discrimination, and undermines the ability of local authorities to challenge the prejudice that exists towards travellers' (Crawley, 2004: 35). However, not all organisations can distinguish between the real and perceived link between Travellers and fly-tipping. The London Borough of Newham (2003) wrote a report on unauthorised encampments and associated illegal activity, and it stated that the Council spent £700,000 per year on fly-tipping and unauthorised encampments. In saying this, the two problems of unauthorised encampments and fly-tipping seem to be inextricably linked. The report does concede that not all incidences of fly-tipping are associated with Travellers, but the central theme of the report is the link between unauthorised encampments and the cost to the environment (and of course the taxpayer) of fly-tipping.

The National Farmers' Union (2003) also looks at the cost of mess and the presumed association with Gypsies and Travellers. The report, called *Britain's Rural Outlaws* says:

> Well equipped, extremely organised and above the law — the problem of illegal travellers is now so bad that the majority of farmers have been affected in some way.
>
> Rural Britain now faces a daily barrage of physical threats, attacks on livestock and crops, dumping of rubbish and illegal encampments that the police are unable or unwilling to act against.
>
> Nearly 80% of farmers questioned by the NFU have suffered at the hands of these 'rural outlaws' over the past five years with the estimated cost to the industry a massive £100 million per year.
>
> (NFU, 2003: 1)

The theme of mess, in the primary research findings, echoes examples cited earlier in the book. For instance, Turner (2002) included 'dirty' as a discursive theme in his work on Gypsies and Travellers. In describing Gypsies and Travellers as messy or dirty, it serves to 'other' them and to heighten their presence in order that surveillance is made easier. The surveillant control is achieved through discourse which continues to define and redefine Gypsies and Travellers as messy and dirty.

The cost of clearing up unauthorised encampments was the strongest theme to come out of the 'negative' reports, in the media analysis exercise. The issue of cost and mess was couched in a way to

tell the reader — 'you are paying for all this through your council tax'.
Examples of this include: 'Mess left by travellers over the last two
years has cost Redditch taxpayers £50,000 to clean up' (*This is
Worcestershire*, 2003: 9). 'Birmingham taxpayers have forked out tens
of thousands of pounds to evict [Travellers] and clear up their mess
and litter' (*Birmingham Evening Mail*, 2003: 5). A headline in one local
newspaper said *£60,000 to keep them out* and it went on to describe the
years of work and the amount of money spent in clearing a green-
field site, and then making it 'traveller-proof' for the future (*This is
Wiltshire*, 2003: 1). Another newspaper carried a similar article in
which it stated that 'On Wednesday Camarthenshire County Council completed a two-day clean-up of the site, removing rubbish —
including nappies and tyres — in an operation reputedly costing
more than £6,000.' (*South Wales Evening Post*, 2003: 2). These examples are representative of many local newspaper articles, this theme
is also demonstrated in national articles. However, media analysts
and groups such as the Gypsy/Traveller Media Advisory Group
(GTMAG) see local newspaper representations of Gypsies and Travellers as some of the most negative in all the media.

The issue of cost and mess is a heated and emotional one. The cost
theme is also reflected in reporting on asylum seekers — especially in
the local press where there are claims that asylum seekers are given
houses and benefits, whilst those local people in need, those who
have often paid taxes, do not secure help from the government. The
issue with Gypsies and Travellers is similar, the public is left feeling
that they are paying taxes for public services, but that those public
services are being exhausted clearing up after Gypsies and Travellers. This theme of cost makes the issue personal to all those who
read the newspaper article (and those who are influenced by the
reader); they feel they are personally paying for something they
don't benefit from and which instead benefits others with
'anti-social' lifestyles. The cost of Gypsies and Travellers raises their
profile in the local vicinity, and not only are the associated costs
monitored and reported on (London Borough of Newham, 2003) but
the sites and the Gypsies and Travellers themselves come under
wider scrutiny, because the local public feels that it must monitor the
condition of the sites, particularly unauthorised sites, so that they
can report to the police or the council and that swift action can be
taken to control the amount of expenditure. The discourse of the cost
of Gypsies and Travellers is a powerful tool to control them. This
'costing' of the lives of Gypsies and Travellers is evident in other

research too. Morris and Clements (2002) looked at the cost of not providing sites, rather than focusing on the cost of provision. They also made the point that a lifestyle could not really have a numerical value placed upon it and indeed, by trying to cost a lifestyle, this heightened the 'otherness' (costliness) of that lifestyle.

Information from the local authority planning consultation exercise also reflected the importance placed on cost and mess. Examples of some of the quotes from previous written objections, provided by the Planning Officer, included:

Public Objections

'What would you think if you bought a £150K house from Barratts to find your neighbours were Gypsies?'

'The value of my property which I work hard to pay for would drop in value overnight. Perhaps the Council would be prepared to compensate people living close to this site.'

'... put them back in [...] Road with a site warden to keep them and the site clean and hygienically tidy.'

'These Travellers contribute nothing, only filth.'

'MESS, <u>THIEVING</u> AND POLLUTION'

'The Police admit they have no control as to when or where they turn up, or any control of Travellers what-so-ever.'

'Surely cost should be one of the most important factors? After all, it's someone else's money you are spending.'

'Looking at the last location near the [...] river, the mess they left, the horses wandering around and the general squalor of the site appals me and we DO NOT want it here.'

'I have first hand experience of Travellers and the carnage they leave behind.'

Figure 7: Public Objections

This list of objections from the public is comparable to the discourse of Czech television debates, outlined by Leudar and Nekvapil (2000). Although the comments from the local authority debate are linked more heavily to cost, the extreme undertone to the discourse is similar.

National newspaper stories did not seem to have a significant, overt, impact on the Gypsies and Travellers in the focus groups. It appeared to be that the local newspaper stories had more resonance, partly because of the immediacy of the effect of the report on their settled neighbours. One particular local article, which had angered the Travellers, was about a funeral of a popular young Traveller man. Instead of some discussion of the qualities of the deceased, as is often the format of a local newspaper article covering a death; the article instead focused on cars outside the church. The main theme was the disruption that had been caused by many cars being parked outside of the church, and it referred to a mess being left behind. The Travellers were furious about this article; they asked what possible mess could be left behind from them parking outside a church for a funeral? There were a lot of cars, but then there can be the same if it were for a young member of the settled community. They felt that mess was associated with Gypsies and Travellers even when most Travellers were clean and tidy. They were aware that articles in the local newspapers, and speeches by local politicians, referred to sites being a mess. However, it was felt that the behaviour of a small minority was used as an excuse to misrepresent all Gypsies and Travellers.

Cost is the most important theme to come out of this research, it links with findings from other empirical research (Morris and Clements 2002) and it is also explained by two of the stages in the theoretical framework outlined in chapter three. 'Cost' is both a theme of discourse that is used as a tool of control; and it is a motive for exercising control. In this regard, it is unique amongst the discursive themes in my research. The other themes tend to be discursive trends that can be linked to the motive to 'other', perhaps in order to save costs. Cost is the only theme that is discursive tool and motive to control, (a 'how' and a 'why' theme) according to the framework.

Labelling – Gypsies or Travellers?

Two newspaper articles, in the media analysis, focused on the distinction between Gypsies and Travellers. Both of these were in fact letters from local people in the settled community and they were negative in their portrayal. In both cases it is not a journalistic article which was analysed, but instead letters printed in local newspapers. The first letter said:

> With reference to 'Travellers' I feel that Penwith has to take a seri-ous firm stand here and not encourage this unlawful residency. As a landowner of Cornish soil and an environmentalist who has worked for 30 years to nurture and protect Cornwall, the idea of Penwith being a safe haven for these people is very saddening.
>
> The title 'Traveller' is a romantic title for a band of people who have not earned the use or warrant of this title.
>
> So why are they called 'Travellers', they don't actually travel anywhere! They hang around on roadsides and waste land …
>
> Some of these people are threatening in their behaviour, aggressive. There may be the odd family group who are genuine but in my experience they don't often 'park up' with larger groups.
>
> Penwith please be realistic, stop calling this group 'travellers' —they're hardly of the Benedict Allen variety of 'Romany Ryes'—gypsies never camp with 'travellers'. Save Penwith from becoming an easy place to doss.

> (*The Cornishman*, 2003a: 35)

As well as marking out a distinction between Travellers and Gypsies —fake and genuine—the author of the article also heightens the Travelling community as 'other'. Terms such as 'these people' followed with negative associated characteristics, again serve to heighten the presence of the Gypsy or Traveller in the local popula-tion and to mark them out for surveillance and control. Terms like 'these people' also link in with the theory of proximity (Bauman, 1989) which is discussed in chapter seven. 'These people', Gypsies and Travellers, are not like 'us' and therefore don't need to be treated with the respect that 'ordinary people' would expect.

The second letter is also negative; and is in response to a previous article.

> Sir,

> I write regarding the recent article, The End of the Road for Trav-ellers in Town. As a resident of Eldene, Swindon, I was very pleased to see you have given our cause some publicity. How-ever, having used the word 'travellers' throughout the first 10 paragraphs, paragraph 11 starts with the words 'the gypsies'.
>
> The people featured in the article are not gypsies. They are travellers.
>
> Gypsies are members of the Romany tribe. They are extremely honest, hard-working and clean. Unlike gypsies, travellers are

thieves, liars, lazy and dirty — as we have learned to our cost here in Eldene.

(Western Daily Press, 2003c: 12)

It is virtually impossible to imagine a published piece of writing about any other ethnic group, describing them as 'thieves, liars, lazy and dirty', being allowed past the editorial control of the newspaper. Why then, does it seem to be acceptable to talk about Gypsies and Travellers in this way? Partly, this can be explained by the success of 'othering' Gypsies and Travellers. Because they are seen as so distant from the settled norm, it is easier to continue to use discriminatory discourse. The writer of the letter also assumes to be blessed with the knowledge that allows them to distinguish between 'real' and 'fake' Gypsies, just by looking at them (Acton, 1994). In providing a distinction, the writer of the letter is making the job of the surveillant society even easier. 'Do not worry about the good traditional Gypsies: concentrate on the dirty, thieving Travellers — they are the ones who need controlling', is what this distinction is saying.

There are additional issues surrounding the labelling of the Travelling community. For instance, there is the colloquialism of the term 'Gypsies'. 'Gypo' is a slang term and it is extremely insulting. Although there have been some examples of reclaiming negative labels for use within the community they are describing (Kennedy, 2002), this has certainly not happened with the term 'Gypo'; indeed it has had an effect on the word Gypsy.

The lack of objection to this language and labelling demonstrates public acquiescence (Zelizer, 1993). Negative labelling of Gypsies and Travellers does not meet resistance from readers or listeners because they are agreeing to the social construction of the 'truth' about Gypsies and Travellers through the discriminatory discourse. There is also a theme of the division between 'real' and 'bogus' in the media discourse on asylum seekers. This division is perceived and it has been central to media and political discussion of asylum seekers for some time. The Evening Standard, in March 2000, ran a feature entitled *Seeking a safe haven*. This seemed to be a sympathetic article looking at how asylum seekers struggled to get on in the UK. However, the article did presume to know the difference between 'cheats' and 'genuine asylum seekers'.

> Never has it been such a bad time to be a genuine asylum seeker. A frenzy of vituperation has been generated against all refugees — in newspapers, among politicians and elsewhere ... But the cheats are a minority. Most asylum seekers, like Matin, a

fresh-faced 16 year old who arrived in London from Afghanistan last November in the back of a smuggler's lorry, are genuine. (McCrystal, 2000: 7)

The above quotation on the reporting of asylum seekers is important here as it provides a comparison with the reporting on Gypsies and Travellers. This comparison was mentioned previously in relation to Turner's (2000) paper. Asylum seekers and Gypsies/Travellers are written about with the use of similar discriminatory characteristics — similar social constructions of the 'truth'.

In the late 1990's and early 2000's the word 'bogus' was being used by central political figures. The term seemed to be used to incite strong feelings out of political motivation. It is impossible to distinguish who started with this term 'bogus' or 'cheat' as opposed to 'genuine' or 'real'. Did the politicians start using these terms and then the newspapers reported them? Or did the newspapers use the terms and the politicians picked up on them being popular terms that would portray the message? Either way it seems to be accepted that there are 'cheats' and then there are 'genuine' asylum seekers; and that politicians and journalists can tell just by looking at someone which is the case.

Mayall (2004) discusses the issue of labelling and Gypsies and Travellers. One of the problems he identifies is the dual definition of Gypsies and Travellers according, on the one hand, to race, and on the other, to nomadism. This confusion in political and legal terminology exacerbates the problem of labelling in other areas of discourse, such as media debate.

This distinction between genuine and non-genuine is certainly an issue for Gypsies. The traditional 'Roma' Gypsies are seen as 'proper' Gypsies with their painted wagons and traditional way of life. Travellers are seen to be less honest and are perceived to be thieves and cheats with a tendency to create a mess on common lands. This distinction is based upon perception and it is exaggerated in the media.

Influx and Invasion

One example of this discursive theme is from the *Western Daily Press* article 'The End of the Road for Travellers in Town'. The article quotes a local councillor as saying 'Hopefully, after all these years, we'll finally see an end to the illegal invasions which have caused so much misery and anger in this area.' (*Western Daily Press*, 2003b: 25). Taken out of context of the article, this quote from a local councillor

could be referring to a war zone—'illegal invasions' is strong terminology to describe unauthorised encampments.

The *Grimsby Evening Telegraph* used similar terminology in its
article 'Preparing for an influx of travellers'.

> ... at Christmas, there was just such an occurrence down the
> coast on land owned by East Lindsey District Council at
> Skegness. The authorities were caught unprepared and the
> disturbances that ensued resulted in pubs, restaurants, shops
> and leisure attractions remaining closed for the entire festive
> season.
>
> Although there has never been an influx on such a scale in
> Cleethorpes, the possibility remains—with the latest gathering
> on Grimsby's Freshney Parkway an indication that travellers can
> set up home where and when they want to.
>
> (Wright, 2003: 8)

In addition to the articles using the term 'influx' or 'invasion' there
were more who used other terminology, but which still served the
purpose of antagonising the settled community into thinking that
Gypsies and Travellers were not just invading spaces but going
unpunished for a variety of different anti-social activities. One such
example says:

> However, would he not admit the people he appears to represent
> flout the law persistently in a way that *we ordinary citizens* never
> could and that they have obtained planning permission where
> we would not. Can he not appreciate this rankles with the *ordi-
> nary* taxpayer? (*Bristol Evening Post*, 2003: 10) [*Emphasis added*]

As well as a reference to 'flouting the law' this article clearly marks
the Gypsies and Travellers out as 'other'. Referring to the settled
community as 'ordinary' and 'taxpayers', immediately labels
Gypsies and Travellers as extraordinary—as 'other'. This debate of
otherness is discussed in chapter seven, but it has relevance here in
understanding some of the terms and words, such as 'we ordinary
citizens', which have an impact on Gypsies and Travellers.

Many of the negative press articles on Gypsies and Travellers
used a variety of words to describe Travellers on unauthorised
encampments. Examples of the words which came to light in the
coding process were: 'blight, eyesore, battle, theft, intimidation,
aggression, stand-guard, control and pilfering'. These words and
phrases indicate negative characteristics and are offensive; but are
the newspaper editors wrong to include them? Wright (2003)
includes advice from the Commission for Racial Equality:

Words like 'tinker', 'itinerant' or 'gypo' are all highly offensive to those about whom they are used and should be avoided.

Terms such as 'scroungers', 'dole dodgers' and 'bogus asylum seeker' should only be used when they are accurate descriptions of particular individuals.

(Wright, 2003: 8).

The use of words and themes used in the media about Gypsies and Travellers was debated in the Radio Four programme *The Message* on 6th February 2004. It is the issue of which words are used to negate characteristics of Gypsies and Travellers which is of interest here. The debate in the programme was in response to the 'campaign' by the Express newspaper to stop Gypsies and Travellers 'flooding-in' from the EU accession countries. The guests on the show included Jeremy Dear: the General Secretary of the National Union of Journalists, Dan Tench: a media lawyer, Julian Baggini: Editor of *The Philosopher* magazine and Dr Mark Thompson: freelance consultant and writer. They were discussing the question of when free speech crosses the line and when it may cause incitement to racial hatred. The guests referred to the Public Order Act (this is the Public Order Act 1986, of which Section 17 deals with racial hatred). It was explained that the Public Order Act sets a high test on the incitement to racial hatred and it was extremely difficult to prove; indeed there has never been a test of a newspaper under this piece of legislation. The other safeguard mentioned was the Press Complaints Commission (PCC) Code. The Code does not contain a specific provision on the incitement to racial hatred, but it does include the issue of discrimination. Additionally, it focuses on the accuracy of reports, as a safeguard measure. The issue of accuracy was discussed in relation to the Express campaign. One guest on the programme used the example of the Express suggesting that 1.6 million Gypsies and Travellers would come to Britain. It was argued that there were 1.6 million Gypsies and Travellers in the EU accession countries, but that it was extremely unlikely (and the Express knew it) that every single Gypsy and Traveller would move to Britain. This could be considered as an inaccurate figure, making the Express report inaccurate and therefore contravening the PCC code.

The Radio 4 programme guests also spent time talking about one specific word used in the Express articles — that of 'leech' or 'leeching'. The debaters did agree that the term was offensive but they could not agree that it necessarily gave rise to incitement to racial hatred. One of the guests said that repeated use of racist language does have an effect and that it can actually cause bad consequences for the subjects of the racist language. This is the key point of the present book: that systems of discourse result in actions which can control particular minority groups, in this case Gypsies and Travellers. Another of the guests agreed and said that in their local area — Dover — police were warning local newspapers that the repeated use of racist and offensive language could incite racial hatred. The debaters also talked about the label 'Gypsy' being used as a derogatory term in itself — this is interesting in light of the debate in this section and in relation to the responses from Gypsies and Travellers in the focus groups.

The host of the debate wondered whether it was worrying that the reporting in the Express on Gypsies and Travellers hadn't caused more of a scandal either in the rest of the media or amongst the public. One of the guests felt that it was worrying, but that it was because people don't recognise the reporting for what it is — racist. The guest who lived near Dover agreed that the public didn't recognise this language as racist (and this links in again with Zelizer's [1993] public acquiescence). He said that the Folkestone local press had used inflammatory and racist language about asylum seekers and that this had become part of the local discourse. When interviewing members of the public they used some of the racist newspaper language and themes — such as 'flooding in' and 'invasion' but when asked for examples to back these claims up, they couldn't provide any. Not only does this link with Zelizer (1993) but also with Bauman (1989). The example of local people in Folkestone shows their public acquiescence in the social construction of asylum seekers, in order that there is less guilt in them being treated differently. It is interesting that the social construction of truth takes precedence in the minds of people, even when examples of what happens in everyday practice do not back up this social construction.

The debate then turned to the motive behind such reporting and the agenda of the newspapers was discussed. The anti-Gypsy/Traveller agenda of the Express was demonstrated with the focus of the article being firmly weighted on one side — the views of Gypsies and Travellers were not represented fairly and their views were far outweighed by the negative images portrayed in the newspaper. The agenda was demonstrated, but another guest asked 'what of the motive?' A reply came from a man who had heard from journalists that, in a meeting, the proprietor of the Express newspaper had said that in nine days of consecutive anti-asylum seeker headlines sales had increased by 20,000. This increased sale of newspapers goes some way to explaining the motive in this particular case, but it cannot explain all motives behind other surveillance and discourse measures.

Before the debate finished, the concept of 'free-speech' was discussed. Jenni Murray suggested that free speech could be jeopardised if newspapers were not allowed to print such stories. Guests responded by saying that free-speech was really the freedom of an individual to free speech and that concept was to protect individuals who may be coerced into not expressing themselves. In the case of newspapers and powerful organisations it is not about free speech, but the power to control views (*BBC Radio 4*, The Message, 2004).

The last viewpoint, on the concept of free speech, is central to the debate in this book. The media cannot be seen as simply a 'truthful' reporting mechanism, or a way of reflecting the views of society. Instead it can be seen to construct social truths, and an acquiescent public accept these new truths (Zelizer, 1993); their views can be controlled by the media. The impact of the media on the control and surveillance of Gypsies and Travellers cannot, therefore, be underestimated. It is important to recognise how the media shapes and controls views and how those views in turn shape and control the lives of Black and Minority Ethnic groups, such as Gypsies and Travellers.

A further trend in national media reporting is that of Gypsies and Travellers in the accession countries to the European Union. A variety of scare stories have been used in newspapers and this theme gathered pace early in 2004. The Guardian newspaper included a summary of the situation, entitled *False Figures*:

> A new race scare is running in the media. It began on an inside page of the Sunday Times with a news story suggesting that at least 100,000 Gypsies are expected to arrive in the UK when the European Union expands by 10 states in May … The Sun followed up on Monday with a front page and two inside pages on the tens of thousands of Eastern European Gypsies heading for Britain. By yesterday, the Express was forecasting on its front page that 1.6 million Roma were ready to 'flood in'. (*The Guardian*, 2004: 25)

A story in the Express (which was part of a campaign to get the Government to keep tight immigration controls, such as Spain, France and Germany) stated: *Gypsies: You Can't Come In*. The front page said:

Gypsies planning to come to Britain this May are to be sent packing after Tony Blair finally admitted yesterday that taxpayers face being fleeced.

Mr Blair dramatically dumped Labour's open-door policy after ministers became alarmed by evidence that large numbers of poverty-stricken migrants, including many Roma gypsies, will head for Britain to claim benefits when their countries join the European Union.

The U-turn is a victory for the Daily Express, which has led the way in exposing the scandal.

(O'Flynn, 2004: 1-2)

In an earlier report in January 2004, the campaign had included an article outlining the problems of Gypsies coming to Britain, and it allegedly quoted the view of Express readers.

Secret plans to deal with a massive influx of gipsies from eastern Europe have been drawn up by ministers amid warnings that Britain could be overwhelmed. While publicly claiming Britain will benefit from its open-door policy to 10 new EU member countries, the Government privately fears it could lead to economic disaster. Countries like France, Germany and Spain have taken much tougher stances than the UK, and as a result ministers have prepared emergency powers to contain the potential catastrophe …

The scale of public concern about a predicted 100,000 gipsies coming here from the Czech Republic alone over the next seven years was clear yesterday in a vote by Daily Express readers. In answer to the question 'Should we let gipsies invade Britain?' 98 per cent of people — 16,829 readers — said no …

The number of people removed from Britain is running at a record high of 1,500 a month said a [Home Office] spokeswoman. It was right that immigration law continued to be enforced, she added.

(Baird, 2004: 8)

These reports in the Express newspaper are extreme. Indeed the Express journalists considered reporting their own employer to the Press Complaints Commission. Seventy of the Express staff held a meeting at the National Union of Journalists and expressed that they were uncomfortable with the pressure being placed on them to write 'anti-Gypsy' articles (Kundnani, 2004).

Media Construction of Gypsy/Traveller

It could be argued that the representation of Gypsies and Travellers in the media goes beyond labelling in order to heighten their presence and keep them under surveillance. It could be alleged that the media construct their own Gypsy and Traveller truths. Zelizer (1993) highlights the problem of media construction of 'truth':

> In an age where so few people are able to accomplish primary experience of public events and must instead depend on some degree of mediated experience, the use of narrative to alter realities and construct new ones that better fit the narrator's agenda is a practice with problematic implications. For the success of such a practice is predicated on the acquiescence of publics, publics who accept such preferred constructions as 'real' and accurate. (Zelizer, 1993: 204)

Zelizer refers to the 'narrator's agenda'. This is difficult to ascertain in the reporting of Gypsies and Travellers in the media. For instance, did the Express have an agenda of persuading the public that Gypsies and Travellers were a threat to Britain, and if they did what benefit would that agenda bring the Express? Perhaps the Express felt that its agenda was to reflect the views of the public; if resonant themes and narratives were used perhaps more people would buy and read the newspaper because they agreed with the views. The motive for narrative social construction is an interesting concept and if a view was taken that the Express wanted to reflect and embellish on the views of the public, in order to sell more newspapers then this would tie in more readily with Zelizer's idea of public acquiescence. Although the newspaper may be reflecting the views of the public it is at the same time embellishing upon those views and constructing a new 'truth' about Gypsies and Travellers to further feed the anxieties of the public. However the public has to be ready to accept these new truths for the construction to work.

It is notable how much impact the media has on the 'truth' of a situation and that false or exaggerated representation soon becomes a new 'truth'. This links in with chapter seven which looks at moral panics and folk devils and the place of the Gypsy and Traveller. The lesson for this chapter is that there is a need for monitoring of the media and a requirement for standards and a code of practice which must be enforced, not only by the Press Complaints Commission (PCC), but also by the currently acquiescing public.

The media is regulated by the PCC and journalists should work according to a code of conduct drawn up by the National Union of Journalists. Additionally, the Commission for Racial Equality has also provided guidance for journalists entitled *Travellers, Gypsies and the media* (CRE, 2000). The main areas of the guidance include 'Steer clear of exploiting prejudice', 'Check the facts', 'Don't let your news

agenda only be driven by the way others are handling the issue',
'Look behind the story line', 'Listen to the people you are writing
about', and 'Don't label people if it is not relevant' (CRE, 2000).

Morris (2000) underlines this unfair treatment of Gypsies and
Travellers in the media:

> Yet the print media commonly suggest to their readers, in their
> representations of Travellers, that this category of people rou-
> tinely display certain negative characteristics not only typical of
> but essential to the group: that is, they represent Travellers in a
> stereotypical and prejudicial fashion. The relationship of the rep-
> resentation to the real is the same as it would be for any societal
> group: some Travellers are dishonest or law-breaking, some
> don't clean up after themselves. The difference is that while some
> settled people also have those characteristics, all other settled
> people are not assumed also to possess them, as is the case for
> Travellers. (Morris, 2000: 213)

She goes on to discuss the use of categorisation and stereotyping:

> But while useful as a means of simplifying complex things and
> people, stereotyping is problematic when used by adults to sim-
> plify and therefore more easily deal with things of which they are
> afraid and lack knowledge. If everything they read about the
> object of their fears and ignorance (from childhood books to
> adulthood newspapers) simply confirms their reductive
> assumptions, they are encouraged to continue in this simplistic
> and sometimes prejudicial thinking. Therein lies a major root of
> social exclusion. (Morris, 2000: 215)

Important in Morris' work, and in this research, is the distinction
made between 'good' Gypsy and 'bad' Traveller. This was discussed
earlier on in connection to the distinction made between 'real' and
'bogus' asylum seekers. Morris (2000) claims that often the 'real'
Gypsy is a figment of the imagination. Just as the media and the public can embellish on a negative image, so they can for a positive
image. The 'good' Gypsy is one who wears traditional brightly col-
oured clothing and lives in a painted, horse- drawn caravan; the
'good' Gypsy is mysterious and romantic and 'care-free'. The problem arises when the reality of Gypsies and Travellers does not match
up to romantic myths of 'good' Gypsies. The juxtaposition between
the truth and the myth, as well as the exaggerated representation of
the 'bad' Gypsy in the media, serves to highlight the characteristics
of Gypsies and Travellers and to mark them out as 'other'.

> The 'bad' Gypsy is dirty, thieving, surviving on wits rather than
> skill and so necessarily living outside the mores and laws of set-

tled society, providing a low standard of goods and services to settled people and then using nomadism to 'slip the net' of the law, scrounging and parasitic, living off the scraps and through the loopholes of settled society and taking it for what he or she can get, leaving disgusting piles of human and industrial waste on every piece of land on which he or she has settled, potentially violent, creating expense, fear and conflict by their very nature. This aspect of the so-called Gypsy character is so firmly held by settled people that 'to gyp' has come to mean 'to be cheated', as in 'I've been gypped'. (Morris, 2000: 216)

Perhaps one of the reasons that there has been little response from the Travelling community to their representation in the media, is that firstly there can be an issue of illiteracy and there is also the fact that Travellers may move on if they receive prejudicial treatment and so, sometimes, are not in one place long enough to fight the media representation.

There is an increasing interest, by certain groups, in the representation of Gypsies and Travellers in the media. The newly formed Gypsy & Traveller Media Advisory Group (GTMAG) monitors articles in the press concerning Gypsies and Travellers. The membership of GTMAG consists of Gypsies and Travellers, representatives from the Commission for Racial Equality, Gypsy organisations such as Friends, Families and Travellers; local government and a number of academic institutions are also represented. The main objectives of the group are to monitor and catalogue discriminatory media representation of Gypsies and Travellers, to ensure that discriminatory reporting is brought to the attention of the media regulators and to raise awareness and positively promote Gypsy and Traveller culture and lifestyle (GTMAG, 2003).

The GTMAG is not just an interesting concept on a practical level, it is also of interest in looking back to chapter four on the theories of control. Particularly relevant here is Foucault's (1980) explanation of power as a fluid concept — rather than a fixed zero-sum entity. It has been argued throughout this book that Gypsies and Travellers are controlled by society through techniques of surveillance, as a result of their heightened presence. In a traditional, zero-sum concept of power this would see Gypsies and Travellers as permanently oppressed by the rest of society. Society holds power and control over Gypsies and Travellers and it would seem that the power relationship is heavily skewed against the Travelling community. Perhaps GTMAG represents a turning point in the relationship. Rather than the Gypsies and Travellers being held under surveillance by the media—the media is now under the surveillance of Gypsies and Travellers, to a certain extent. The relationship between the media and GTMAG represents Foucualt's fluidity of power, and it provides a relevant practical example of Marston's (2004) resistance to dominant discourse, as discussed previously. The impact of GTMAG cannot be monitored here as it is still only in its infancy, however this would be interesting research for the future.

Conclusion

Most of the key themes from the analysis of media reporting have been included in this chapter, amongst discussion of a range of media representations of Gypsies and Travellers. In addition, there was an examination of why the media may depict the travelling community in this way, and it was seen that the theme of cost, in addition to being a discursive theme, could also be a motive for 'othering' Gypsies and Travellers.

There are two remaining themes that haven't been discussed in this section on the media. 'Folk devils' is an issue examined in the next chapter, and the analytical theme of 'who is talking about Gypsies and Travellers' is included towards the end of the book.

Chapter Seven

'Society', Moral Panics, Folk Devils, and Gypsies

Introduction

This chapter reflects on the theories of control and discourse, examined earlier in the book, and aims to provide an explanation of why the control of Gypsies and Travellers is seen as necessary. It discusses, in detail, the third part of the three-stage process of control; it looks at why there is a need for control and suggests the motive for the control of Gypsies and Travellers through discourse.

Gypsies and Travellers are undoubtedly perceived as 'other'. There is a large body of work around the issue of 'otherness', and terms such as 'folk-devil' and deviant are used by authors including Cohen (1980). It is important to remember that the labelling of someone as 'deviant' or 'other' is not a benign statement. The analysis of discourse theory, earlier, demonstrated that by saying something, one can socially construct something. Therefore, by labelling Gypsies and Travellers as 'other', society is actually making them 'other'; they are constructing their identity as different, and focus on differences, rather than similarities. Why is this done? I argue that it can be a tool to control the person(s) being labelled. It can also be seen as a tool to control society as a whole; for instance, through raising the fear of 'others' the government could make the population more accepting of political changes.

Dandeker (1990) reviewed Cohen's (1980) notion of a shift in the structures of surveillance and social control, which included a shift from:

> ... establishing causal knowledge about the mental processes of deviants in favour of, on the one hand, neo-classical and justice models which emphasize 'just' punishment for offences committed by *morally responsible individuals*, and, on the other, more behaviourist models which eschew explanation in favour of

programmes for the control of deviancy that simply 'work'.
(Dandeker, 1990: 146) [*Emphasis added*]

There is a clear distinction, made by Dandeker, between 'morally responsible individuals' and 'deviants'. This chapter examines what is meant by 'deviant' by analysing what is meant by 'society', and it makes the links between deviants and Gypsies/Travellers. Cohen and Young (1973) state that it is important to look at:

> ... the conceptions of deviance and social problems revealed in the mass media and the implicit view of society behind such conceptions. (Cohen and Young, 1973: 10)

I will follow the advice of Cohen and Young (1973) and examine 'conceptions of deviance and social problems' in order to provide context and explanation.

'Society'

Society means different things to different people in a variety of circumstances. However, one possible meaning of society refers to 'society as a whole'. Here society includes differing individuals and groups, and incorporates, or tries to control, their different norms and ideals. In this way society is seen as abstract. It is an entity which can be joined by deciding to contract in, or something to be excluded from if 'societal' norms are not adhered to.

Current government thinking would seem to support this theory of society as abstract. The Labour Government is responsible for a raft of 'social inclusion' initiatives, aimed at bringing everyone into 'society'. Margaret Thatcher once argued that 'there is no such thing as society'; she went on to qualify this by stating:

> My meaning, clear at the time, but subsequently distorted beyond recognition, was that society was not an abstraction, separate from the men and women who composed it, but a living structure of individuals, families, neighbours and voluntary associations ... (Thatcher, 1993: 626)

Often society can be taken to mean an entity. It is referred to as something with which people interact and are involved in or excluded. However, I would argue that society is not an abstraction, rather it is to do with the relationships between people and organisations, structures and agencies, — the imbrication of men and things (Foucault, 1994). Indeed society is not one 'whole' but a mixture of structures and sub-structures: groups of societies. The word society denotes a commonality of the people and structures within it.

However, it is not possible to assume a commonality of norms amongst, for instance, all the people in England. The current government seems to assume that there is a society at large and that there are societal norms to which everyone must conform or be excluded.

Berger and Luckmann (1966) talk about society as both objective and subjective reality:

> Since society exists as both objective and subjective reality, any adequate theoretical understanding of it must comprehend both these aspects. As we have already argued, these aspects receive their proper recognition if society is understood in terms of an ongoing dialectical process composed of the three moments of externalization, objectivation and internalization. (Berger and Luckmann, 1966: 149)

This links in with the examination of Foucault's internalisation of the gaze, discussed in chapter four. Berger and Luckmann continue to look at the theory of society as subjective reality, and they say:

> When the generalized other has been crystallized in consciousness, a symmetrical relationship is established between objective and subjective reality. What is real 'outside' corresponds to what is real 'within'. Objective reality can readily be 'translated' into subjective reality, and vice versa. Language, of course, is the principal vehicle of this ongoing translating process in both directions. (Berger and Luckmann, 1966: 153)

Berger and Luckmann define society as subjective reality which, through language, links in with 'objective' reality — each defining the other. Not only is this useful in thinking about what society means, but it shows the links between society, the gaze and discourse. It helps to explain how the objective 'reality' of Gypsies and Travellers is internalised into subjective reality, but then enters a dialectical process with objective reality again; a cycle of definition and social construction of reality continues.

Although there is an assumption of 'society' as a whole, it must be recognised that it is made up of groups of people with different perceived norms. These norms are sometimes constructed from outside; or they are a set of values which honestly reflect the values of the group or individual. Although the differences between members of society is spoken of in more sensitive terms in the 21st century, the following quote serves as an illustration of perceived norms:

> In the first place there is the artisan element. Members of this class are in receipt of fair wages. As a rule they are steady, thrifty and socially ambitious. They are good tenants ...

> The next step in the gradation is occupied by individuals who have not mounted quite so high in the social scale. One section has been unfortunate, and ... has become discouraged ... The other includes those prone to be lazy or careless, and those who are not particularly intelligent or ambitious or are possessed of bad habits ...
>
> The third section includes the incorrigible, the drunkard, the criminal, the immoral, the lazy, and the shiftless ... as Lord Shaftesbury significantly remarks, they have hardly any domestic or civilized feelings ...
>
> (US Commissioner for Labour, 1895: 439-42
> cited in Harloe, 1995: 21-2)

Although the language in this quotation is not the sort of language one would expect of politicians today, similarities of concept can be found in the work of Murray (1990 & 1994) and his views on the 'Underclass'. Additionally, I found that there are still politicians who use such language, which is discriminatory and racist—the example of MP Andrew MacKay, speaking in the House of Commons in 2002, was referred to at the very beginning of the book.

There has been much work on social exclusion and the characteristics of those that are excluded. This usually focuses on economic differences or inequality of access to goods and services due to ethnicity, gender or age, for instance (Morris & Winn, 1990). Murray's underclass is different to these examinations of social exclusion in that there is a feeling of 'otherness' about those excluded—it is not down to wealth, but instead attitudes and group norms. There are current examples of those who could be categorised as Murray's underclass; they are groups that tend to be vilified by the politicians and the press for not sharing social norms. Gypsies and Travellers are certainly able to be categorised as underclass from the discourse about them in the press and the House of Commons. Words such as 'anti-social', 'nuisance', 'trouble', 'problem', and 'alternative lifestyle' mark them out for such categorisation. Other examples include young single mothers (they became pregnant on purpose in order to jump the queue for a council house—see the Conservative Party Manifesto 2001, in Watt, 2001), economic migrants (not 'real' asylum seekers but those wishing to benefit from England's job market or welfare system—this was a topical issue in the media in the first half of 2001, see Brockes, 2001; and in political rhetoric, see Risman, 2002), indeed council tenants as a whole tend to have a stigma attached to them which smacks of 'underclass'.

If Blair and the US Commissioner for Labour were talking today about societal norms, they would both agree that the norms for the whole of society would relate to the first and part of the second group — e.g. the artisans and the unfortunate who have not been able to scale to the top group in society. The lazy, incorrigible, immoral and drunkard people are assumed to have norms that are not relevant to the good of society as a whole and therefore these perceived norms are not included in the social contract. Everyone in society must aspire to the norms of being employed, settled in a home, hard working, steady and ambitious. Everyone must want to do better all of the time — one should not rest on one's laurels — this is for the incorrigible and lazy. Indeed Prescott, in an article about the Social Exclusion Unit for the Guardian, wrote:

> We [the government] now place emphasis on 'joining up' policy between government departments and taking a long-term approach, applying three basic principles: *reintegration, prevention and mainstreaming*. (Prescott, 2002: 4-5) [*Emphasis added*]

These three methods of reintegration, prevention and mainstreaming are a controlling mechanism focused on the ideal of 'society'. There is a plethora of schemes, initiated by the Social Exclusion Unit, in an attempt to keep people focused on the norms of society and to prevent them from 'dropping out' or being excluded by society. In this sense, society is seen as a club from which one may be barred for bad behaviour.

Although 'society' can be viewed as an abstract structure, to which individuals should aspire to be a part, it can also be used as a way of highlighting those who do not work towards the good of the whole. In this way, the term society is a means of demonstrating who is not 'in' society and it has a function to highlight those in need of additional surveillance.

In chapter four, Foucault's analogy of the gaze was examined as a tool of control. The gaze, surveillance, would not be effective if there were not specific individuals or groups defined as 'other' and isolated from society. How would one know who to watch if they were not pointed out? In the earlier quote from the US Commissioner, the lazy and the incorrigible were pointed out as not valuing the same norms as those steady, hard working artisans. The artisans are alright, he was saying, we need to keep an eye on the lazy and incorrigible though.

Although Foucault's approach and the three-dimensional view of power (Lukes 1974) have been the focus of the discussion on theories of power and control so far, there are noticeable elements of the traditional zero-sum model (one-dimensional view) present in the current system of government in this country. Successive governments fight to win and maintain power and, to a degree, set the rules and define terms in society. There is a multi-directional flow of power and the majority of the population can vote governments in, and lobby them for improvements in the law and in public services. However, once a government is in office it has power to make law and policy and to define societal issues and themes through its own governmental discourse. Therefore, when the government talks about social inclusion it is important to know what it means by the term society.

Whilst Thatcher placed much more responsibility on the individual and the family, and did not really hold with society as an abstract entity (Thatcher, 1993), Prime Minister Blair has a much more inclusive emphasis. It seems that Blair would like everyone to be a stakeholder of this society. Under his leadership there have been ideologies and programmes such as 'Social Inclusion' (Social Exclusion Unit 1998 & 2004), 'New Deal for Communities' (Social Exclusion Unit, 2001), and 'Action Zones' in health and education aimed at reducing social divisions and inequalities (for an example see Barnes *et al.* 2003). All are aimed at including people in 'society'. This has to mean that whilst there is an assumption of 'society' as a whole; there are people who are outside of 'society', as defined by the government. Despite these early social inclusion programmes, it should be noted that the Labour government seems increasingly intent on highlighting those seen as 'outside of society'. One example of this is the emphasis on the increased use of anti-social behaviour orders, which were provided for in the Anti-Social Behaviour Act (2003).

Indeed it may be easier to explain what society means by discovering who is considered to be outside of it, and why. Through reading a variety of policies from the Social Exclusion Unit (1998, 2001, 2004), as well as examining the groups that local authorities, through the Supporting People programme (which came into force in April 2003) are focusing on, the following groups can be seen to be socially excluded:

Example of Socially Excluded Groups

- Black and Minority Ethnic people
- Single mothers
- Offenders
- Homeless
- Unemployed
- Disabled
- 'Social' housing tenants (paradoxically)
- Asylum seekers
- Gypsies and Travellers

Figure 8: Example of Socially Excluded Groups

Each of these groups has different ideals and different perceived norms, as discussed earlier. It is difficult, then, for each of these groups to be included (or controlled) by a single set of societal meta-norms. The above (figure 8) does not show an exhaustive list, but it is sufficient to start a debate on who is included and excluded in the government's view of society.

There is a further issue as to whether, or why, it is left to the government to decide/define what society is and who is excluded from it. This boils down to a fundamental question of democracy — do governments lead the public, or does public opinion lead government action? Blair refers to himself as 'running the country' when in fact he can only say that he is running the administrative centre of operations. Does Blair lead the public, or does he bow to public opinion? The government's own perception of the power they hold over society needs to be considered here in the discussion on the importance of the government definition of society. If one looks at a traditional view of government, such as the example of captaining a ship discussed in the examination of Foucault (1994) in chapter four, it is possible to see why government should define society. If governing society is like managing a ship then it is up to government to manage the role that everyone has; how each individual's functioning and capability can be utilised for the best possible outcome. Being part of society depends on the role that you play within it. John F Kennedy, in his inaugural speech (January 1961), said: 'Ask not what your country can do for you—ask what you can do for your country.' In this respect of governing a country being similar to captaining a ship, a person is involved in society if they are contributing to the smooth running of it. If no contribution is made then it is deemed that certain people or groups are outside of society, as far as the government is concerned. This is problematic, as those who do not have the capability to contribute towards society are excluded from it. It is also tied up in the issue that there is a sub-society, or as Murray termed it 'Underclass'. Those perceived, by government, to be outside of 'society' are viewed as strangers to those who conform to societal norms. They are the subject of, often unwarranted, panic and subsequent surveillance.

Social Norms

This brief section will help with an understanding of 'society' and it also acts as a bridge, in this book, between the evaluation of what society means and an examination of moral panics. Social norms can be almost ethereal, precision is difficult. Some of the most interesting work in the area of social norms is by Elster (1989). He attempts to explain social norms as something concrete and real:

> Rational action is concerned with outcomes. Rationality says, 'If you want to achieve Y, do X'. By contrast, I define social norms by the feature that they are *not outcome-oriented*. The simplest social norms are of the type 'Do X', or 'Don't Do X'. More complex norms might say, 'Do X if it would be good if everyone did X' ...
> For norms to be *social*, they must be (a) shared by other people and (b) partly sustained by their approval and disapproval. Some norms, like norms against cannibalism or incest, are shared by all members of society. Other norms are more group specific ... The other respect in which these norms are *social* is that other people are important for enforcing them, by expressing their approval and, especially, disapproval.

(Elster, 1989: 98-99)

Elster's (1989) view on the importance of public opinion in explaining social norms is relevant to Gypsies and Travellers. It is almost acceptable that there is a way of life outside of the 'settled' population—as long as it is not physically evident. Unfortunately, this seems to be true even in reformist policy. An example of this can be seen in the Traveller Law Reform Bill (2002) which, in Schedule 2 to the Bill, said:

Keep groups small and inconspicuous. Anything more than six
vehicles is likely to be a problem but this will depend on the site
and proximity to other properties. (Traveller Law Reform Bill,
2002, Schedule 2, paragraph 1)

The Bill clearly tells Gypsies and Travellers to be inconspicuous, not
to offend public opinion and meta-societal norms. Unfortunately,
the Bill failed, but campaigners continue to lobby the government
for a Commission and for a duty on local authorities to provide sites.

So far, the discussion in this section on norms has focused on the
wider 'social norms', for instance norms that are accepted by all of
society. However, just as sociologists would not examine 'society' as
a whole but instead examine particular groups, so it must be for the
examination of social norms. Micro-norms apply to particular
groups, and they are unique to that group. For instance, Gypsies and
Travellers see being 'on the road' as a norm. Living in a permanent
dwelling is not a Gypsy norm.

If you lived in a house, you wouldn't have so many friends
around you for a start, you'd be isolated, 'cos we've got different
ways from the house dwellers and we're just used to that way.
(F1, Irish Traveller on LA site, quote from Niner, 2002: 38)

There are many other examples of group micro-norms. An example
includes young children in school belonging to a rebellious 'cool'
group of kids, who would not want to be seen doing homework and
abiding by rules, as they would not gain social acceptance within the
group. The micro-norm for this group of school children is to
disobey school rules and to buck the meta-norm of working hard to
achieve an end goal. Another example may relate to anti-social
youth on a crime-ridden estate, where a security tag or an anti-social
behaviour order (ASBO) is a badge of honour.

Deviance and Moral Panics

Stanley Cohen studied moral panics in his work entitled *Folk Devils
and Moral Panics: The Creation of the Mods and Rockers* (1980). His work
is born largely from the sociology of deviance. Wilkins (1973)
attempts to explain perceptions of deviance and the importance of
information:

As another example of the influence of information on the perception of normality, consider the following experience of the
author. Rather late one Saturday evening he was returning to his
home from central London. He joined a bus queue, which
seemed to him to consist of some six or seven tough and probably

delinquent gang members. He inferred this from the way they stood, and particularly from the manner of their dress. They had not spoken. His knowledge of the delinquent sub-culture did not relieve him of certain feelings of anxiety, or at least of a defensive attitude towards the members of the group. However, immediately they spoke he was able to completely modify his perception of 'abnormality' or deviance of the group — they spoke in French. From his knowledge of the habitual dress of French youth on holiday in England, he was able to fit this apparently 'deviant' behaviour and dress symbolism into a 'normal' or expected context. It would seem, therefore, that we may claim that what is defined as deviant is determined by our subjective experience of 'non-deviant' or 'normal', but that our experience and the resulting classifications can be changed by certain types of information. (Wilkins, 1973: 23)

This example of the definition of deviancy is now over 30 years old, but the premise of the explanation still holds today. The importance of information, on the perception of deviancy can be used in an example of Gypsies and Travellers. The very words Gypsy or Traveller create perceptions of deviance or an element of being 'anti-social'. However, particularly in the media, distinctions are made between 'real' Romany Gypsies and 'fake' Travellers; this is often done through reference to the clothes that are worn, or the wagons driven. Sometimes the term 'smartly dressed' is used to denote respectability and normality; to distinguish 'real' Gypsies from 'deviants' (Thorpe, 2002). This has the same effect as Wilkins hearing the youths speaking French in the earlier example, the information changed his perception of the level of deviancy.

This sociology of deviance is evident in the work of Durkheim, especially his research into suicides (1989). However, there has been more work on this sociology by Becker (1964):

The conventional style of studying deviance has focused on the deviant himself and has asked its questions mainly about him. Who is he? Where did he come from? How did he get that way? Is he likely to keep on being that way? The new approach sees it as always and everywhere a process of interaction between at least two kinds of people: those who commit (or are said to have committed) a deviant act and the rest of society, perhaps divided into several groups itself. The two groups are seen in a complementary relationship. One cannot exist without the other; indeed, they are functions of one another in the strict mathematical sense of quantities whose value depends on the value of other quantities. (Becker, 1964: 2)

This sociology of deviance, according to Becker, fits well with Foucault's theory of control discussed in chapter four. For instance, the deviance described by Becker is not one dimensional – that person is deviant, there is something wrong with them. Instead it relies on at least two, if not three, dimensions of control to explain the sociology of deviance. For instance, it takes the travelling community to define the settled community, and vice versa. The majority of the population in England live in bricks and mortar accommodation, therefore anyone who doesn't do this is seen as 'deviant'. If the majority did not settle, then travelling would not be seen as 'deviant'.

It is important to understand some of the theories of deviancy that were being mooted at a similar time to Cohen's work on folk devils. Cohen (1980) explains reactions to groups and events, and he aims to help understand why and how the panics are started, and indeed who starts them:

> The level for explaining labelling, societal reaction or moral panic is shifted from social control agencies or cultures – or vague allusions to the 'wider society' – to the specific operation of the state. This means relating the working of the moral panic – or the mobilization of public opinion, the orchestration by the media and public figures of an otherwise inchoate sense of unease – to overall political shifts. (Cohen, 1980: xxiii-xxiv)

In other words the mobilisation of a panic is not just accidental; it serves to concentrate the political power of the state. Cohen uses Gramsci's concept of hegemony as a theory to underline this assertion:

> Hegemony denotes the moment when the ruling class is able not merely to coerce its subordinates to conform, but to exercise the sort of power which wins and shapes consent, which frames alternatives and structures agendas in such a way as to appear natural. (Cohen, 1980: xxiv)

Cohen's work argues that the use of moral panics has become more sophisticated since his case study of the Mods and the Rockers. He states that the old sequence, where a specific event triggered a panic, a moral enterprise – followed by mobilisation of control culture – is now gone. In its place a general sense of disquiet is created:

> The control culture is mobilized in advance, real events being anticipated and taken to confirm and justify the need for gradual ideological repression. (Cohen, 1980: xxiv)

This theory does take a rather sinister and negative view of the state's role in the creation and use of moral panics. The use of state control is necessary in an orderly society; the entire premise of the social contract (Rousseau, 1994) is that in 'opting in' to society one agrees to adhere to the rules, which will better life for the majority of society. Cohen's moral panics theory sees governments shaping and controlling behaviour in order to retain and increase their power.

Folk Devils and the Theory of Proximity

Folk devils are the focus of moral panics. In Cohen's (1980) study these were groups of 'youth' — Mods and Rockers. Cohen helps to describe the term folk devil:

> But the groups such as the Teddy Boys and the Mods and Rockers have been distinctive in being identified not just in terms of particular events (such as demonstrations) or particular disapproved forms of behaviour (such as drug-taking or violence) but as distinguishable social types. (Cohen, 1980: 9)

Therefore, the folk devil is not necessarily seen in context of a type of behaviour. Instead, some group members may have helped to define the group but then the media/society/state define the whole group as a particular social type.

There is a plethora of folk devils that goes beyond Cohen's case study; for example the Gypsies. In old-wives' tales Gypsies stole babies; according to Anne Widdecombe they steal pets (see Turner, 2002) and according to the local people in the planning consultation exercise, they are murderers (consultation exercise, 2004). The role of Gypsies and Travellers as folk devils is played out in government policy decisions and is reinforced by the media. The government, for instance, uses the role of Gypsy as folk devil from a functionalist perspective in order to tell the rest of society how not to live. It has been said, previously, that folk devils are played out by government and reinforced by the media, but it is equally likely that they are represented unfairly by the media and this is reinforced by government policy (as was seen in the Express 'campaign' against East European Roma, 2004). Rather than the government and the media having a unilateral relationship, it is suggested that it is a cyclical, mutually re-enforceable one.

Society needs folk devils to be different; we need distance between 'us' and 'them'. Folk devils are created in order that the government, or society as a whole, can say 'they are not like us, they can be treated differently'. If folk devils are punished severely, or treated in an inhumane way, then their definition as folk devil absolves those involved in their treatment, of guilt. If everyone was recognised equally it would not allow people to be treated differently. If a folk devil is marked out as different then it allows 'society' to be comforted that it is alright to treat them in a different way to the way they would like to be treated. A good reference in this area of how a group of people can be treated inhumanely, without causing guilt, is the work of Zygmunt Bauman *Modernity and the Holocaust* (1989). A central theme of this work, which looks at how the Germans treated the Jews, is the issue of proximity. Bauman says that Germans found it difficult to single out Jews that were their neighbours and their work colleagues. The Nazis had to remove them from the proximity of daily neighbourliness—remove them from the social—for everyday Germans to see the Jews as different and therefore subject to the horrors that were fated by the Nazis. The issue of proximity is important in understanding folk devils of all kinds, from asylum seekers to Gypsies.

Bauman (1989) explains the importance of proximity:

> Being inextricably tied to human proximity, morality seems to conform to the law of optical perspective. It looms large and thick close to the eye. With the growth of distance, responsibility for the other shrivels, moral dimensions of the object blur, till both reach the vanishing point and disappear from view. (Bauman, 1989: 192)

For Gypsies and Travellers, this law of proximity can be seen to work. Gypsies can be 'moved on' after 28 days, according to the Criminal Justice and Public Order Act (1994). They are not allowed to 'settle' on certain unauthorised sites and yet there are not enough authorised sites to accommodate them. This bureaucracy is effective in maintaining a distance between 'us' and 'them'. The distance allows society to believe they are not like 'us' and its conscience remains clear when Gypsies and Travellers are treated badly either by the public, the press or the government. The distance created between Gypsies and 'us' has allowed them to become folk devils, and allows them to be treated differently without too much introspection and troubled conscience.

Bauman, in his description of the treatment of Jews (and it should be remembered that Gypsies and Travellers were also killed, in great number, in the Holocaust—see Kenrick, 1999), says:

> This neutralizing, isolating and marginalizing was an achievement of the Nazi regime deploying the formidable apparatus of modern industry, transport, science, bureaucracy, technology.

> Without them, the Holocaust would be unthinkable ... (Bauman, 1989: 188)

Using the 'formidable apparatus' discussed above, the Jews were, step-by-step excluded from German society and turned into folk devils. Bauman discusses the work of another theorist, that of Raul Hilberg. He examines Hilberg's steps that led to the exclusion and destruction of the Jews:

Definition

Dismissals of employees and expropriation of business firms

Concentration

Exploitation of labour and starvation measures

Annihilation

Confiscation of personal effects.

(Bauman, 1989: 190)

These steps are obviously extreme. In the early 21st century in England it is not likely that the sequence would be followed through to its logical conclusion for Gypsies and Travellers; however there is the historical evidence of their being victims of the holocaust (Kenrick, 1999). The steps have been included to serve as an illustrative example of the treatment of 'others' within the theory of proximity. A recent example, which does follow some of Hilberg's steps, is found in the Czech Republic. In a documentary entitled *Gypsies, Tramps and Thieves?* (Channel 4, 2000) the treatment of Gypsies in the Czech Republic was shown. One of the main messages that came over in the programme was not that Gypsies were treated unfairly and cruelly by sections of the Czech population, but that it was state sanctioned. One case was shown where a Gypsy man had been killed, by the 'skinheads', and although there was evidence of their guilt, the alleged perpetrators were not convicted of the killing. Most 'house-dwelling' Czech citizens answered questions about the Gypsies in a derogatory fashion; they felt that they got what was coming to them. One lone voice amongst this group stood out, he said that 'Skinheads are carrying out ethnic cleansing for the Government.' This seemed to be an example of skin heads carrying out action, which defined Gypsies as unworthy, and without going through all of Hilberg's steps it did end with killing. The fact that some of the skinheads felt they were acting on behalf of their country, and that the Czech population and the Gypsies also felt this, makes it a good example of Hilberg's model as discussed by Bauman

(1989). A further example (McLaughlin, 2005) is the Gypsy women in the Czech Republic who undergo forced sterilisation. This has been spoken of by Eastern European Roma previously, but the report in the Observer details the sterilisation programme that is still happening (presumably with state approval) today.

The above steps are discussed in great detail by Bauman; a summary of the discussion demonstrates the main points:

> Definition sets the victimized group apart ... Dismissals and expropriations ... the victimized group is now effectively removed from sight; ... Concentration completes this process of distantiation ... Exploitation and starvation perform a further, truly astonishing, feat: they disguise inhumanity as humanity ... And thus the final act, annihilation, was in no way a revolutionary departure. It was so to speak, a logical ... outcome of the many steps taken before. (Bauman, 1989: 191-2)

Only certain sections of these steps can be taken from Bauman's work and used to explain other groups of folk devils in modern society. Although Gypsies, like Jews, have faced torture and annihilation in their history, it is not something that happens in the 21st century in England. There are still aspects of these steps that can be useful though—the main one being definition. It will help to turn back to Bauman's explanation of this step, in more depth:

> Definition sets the victimized group apart (all definitions mean splitting the totality into two parts—the marked and the unmarked), as a *different* category, so that whatever applies to it does *not* apply to all the rest. By the very act of being defined, the group has been targeted for *special* treatment; what is proper in relation to 'ordinary' people must not necessarily be proper in relation to it. Individual members of the group become now in addition exemplars of a type; something of the nature of the type cannot but seep into their individualized images, compromise the originally innocent proximity, limit its autonomy as the self-sustained moral universe. (Bauman, 1989: 191)

Bauman is not alone in his examination of the idea of proximity. Riggins (1997) discusses this concept in relation to the 'rhetoric of othering'. Riggins also links in with the issue of the politicisation and official sanctioning of othering that takes place in society.

> ... the perception of difference is influenced by economic and political motives ... The rhetoric of Othering dehumanizes and diminishes groups, making it easier for victimizers to seize land, exploit labour, and exert control while minimizing the complicating emotions of guilt and shame. (Riggins, 1997: 9)

The theme of 'folk devils' was evident in my primary research. During a conversation with an officer from the local authority undergoing the planning consultation, the image of Gypsies and Travellers as 'other', as folk devils, was discussed. From historical information on site provision, it became apparent that there had been an issue with one particular site. Originally this was populated and managed by Romany Gypsies, but the Gypsy manager then left and Irish Travellers started to move in. The Romanies and Irish were not at ease with each other and the Romany Gypsies left. At the same time, the previously unpopulated surrounding area started to build up both commercially and residentially:

> As a result the two communities were thrown together. Interest-ingly, if you talk to people today there are a lot of urban myths of how bad the Travellers were, from murders to eating people's pets. At the time however, very few complaints were raised. Without a doubt the criticism of Travellers has grown over the intervening years.
>
> Local populations have difficulty in distinguishing between unauthorised camping and staying on an authorised site. They assume that Travellers are all dirty and trouble. Quite clearly the majority of residents have a prejudice related to Travellers which is now being fuelled by stories that have either no evidence or no way of determining who could have been responsible.

> (Planning Officer, 2004)

This negative discourse, which is not backed up by evidence, is similar to the experience of the Radio 4 debater (discussed in the previous chapter), in his examination of people's views on asylum seekers in Folkestone. The socially constructed truth through dis-course replaces any evidence in reality.

The history of people's views of Travellers helped to contextualise the objections raised by the public in the consultation exercise, and the views of local people seemed to categorise Gypsies and Travel-lers as folk devils. It is interesting to see that the views have become more extreme in the years since the site was closed. This links again with Bauman's theory of proximity (1989) which discusses the 'othering' of a group of people in order that the perpetrator of dis-crimination feels less guilty as they are 'not like us'. There are also links with Morris' research (2000 and 2002) into categorisation and stereotyping. It seems that the more extreme the characteristic — murdering, eating pets — the less like 'normal' settled members of the community Gypsies and Travellers are. This makes it easier for the settled community to deny them decent homes, access to schools or welcoming neighbours. The myth of local discourse, as with the socially constructed 'truth' of the media, is so strong that they cannot remember the reality. For instance, the local people in the planning consultation exercise did not make many complaints when Travellers were actually living on the site, but with hindsight and distance in time there is a new truth that they murdered people and ate people's pets.

There has been some research conducted in Scotland which looks at views of Travellers sites, which may back up this theory of proximity. Duncan (1996) examined neighbour's views of three proposed sites for Travellers. He examined public opposition to the planning permission, and then revisited some of the complainants to ask their views after the site had been up and running for a while:

> We have to conclude that the three sites which were the subject of this study have had far less impact on their 'neighbours' than these people anticipated before the sites were set up. The picture we obtained is that the sites have generally fitted into their chosen surroundings better than people living in the neighbourhood anticipated …
>
> It would be fair to say that our study backs up the view that official sites do settle down to a large extent after they are developed. In none of the sites examined were the number and intensity of objections an appropriate response in retrospect.
>
> (Duncan, 1996: 14)

The Gypsies and Travellers that the Scottish neighbours were objecting to were the mythical messy, costly, troublesome Travellers that are the subject of local discourse and media social construction. However, the Gypsies and Travellers who actually populated the three sites were, not like the people the neighbours had been imagining. The reality was not as bad as the myth. Once the Gypsies and Travellers were seen to be human and were accepted as neighbours, the complaints were not as regular or as rigorous as had been expected. The 'otherness' of the Gypsies and Travellers was less marked.

The stereotyping of Gypsies and Travellers as folk devils was discussed, in the theoretical framework, as part of the motive behind the media's negative discourse. Erjavec (2001) also found this in her empirical work, of their representation in the Slovenian media. She found that unless they were stereotyped, they were not newsworthy. The Gypsy as costly and messy sells more newspapers than the Gypsy who is represented as 'normal'. This motive is reiterated by the research of Clark and Campbell (2000).

It is worth reviewing a quote from Shuinear (1997) discussed earlier in the book:

> ... Gaujos need Gypsies to *personify* their own faults and fears, thus lifting away the burden of them.
>
> This need is so overpowering that time after time, in place after place, Gaujos create situations forcing Gypsies to fill this role.
>
> It is important to remember that what we're talking about here are not 'alien' faults and problems but *Gaujo's own*; therefore, the people onto whom these are projected must be clearly distinct from the Gaujo mainstream, but not utterly foreign to it: *just as in cinema, the screen must be neither too close nor too distant if the image projected onto it is to remain sharply focused.*

(Shuinear, 1997: 27) [*Emphasis added*]

The notion of proximity for Shuinear, in relation to Gypsies and Travellers, is not that the travelling community should be distanced so much that they are out of sight completely. Instead, it is suggested that they should be distant and 'different' enough for there to be reduced moral dilemma about their treatment; but near enough to serve a function, to take the fears and the problems of the Gaujo.

It is important to put this part of the chapter into a current context of control. For instance, it is not really possible to be writing on social control, and which groups are being controlled, without at least acknowledging the events of September 11th, 2001, which saw the beginning of atrocities in New York and Washington, Bali, Nigeria and Madrid. This section does not intend to cover the treatment of minority groups in the US and Britain post 9/11 in any great detail — but it cannot be ignored either. The reason that it is important to look at politics and control post 9/11 is that asylum seekers (which includes some Gypsies and Travellers, particularly from Eastern Europe) are increasingly seen as 'other' in English society. They are seen as different to English nationals and there is an assumption by some parts of the population and by the press, that asylum seekers pose a threat to an 'English' way of life.

The identity of the stranger in society, post 9/11, is important to recognise in this context. However, it is beyond the parameters of this book to provide an in-depth analysis of the effects of 9/11 on society and how minorities are now treated as 'other'. A variety of publications look at this issue, see for instance Sardar (2002), Johnston (2002), Dodd (2002) and Blunkett (2002).

Conclusion

> ... the countryside, it seems, belongs to the middle class, to land-
> owners and to people who engage in blood sports ... This case
> suggests how a group, like New Age Travellers, can be denied a
> place in society through a particular construction of place. A
> rigid stereotype of place, the English countryside, throws up
> discrepant others ... These groups are other, they are folk-devils,
> and they transgress only because the countryside is defined as a
> stereotypical pure space which cannot accommodate difference.
>
> (Sibley, 1995: 107-8, quoted in Cloke et al 2002: 75)

Theories on society, 'otherness' and folk-devils have been explored
in this chapter in order to provide a motive for the control of Gypsies
and Travellers through discourse. As Shuinear (1997) states, Gypsies
and Travellers need to be made 'other' by Gaujos in order to lift away
the burden of their own faults and fears:

> ... the people onto whom these [faults and fears] are projected
> must be clearly distinct from the Gaujo mainstream, but not
> utterly foreign to it ... (Shuinear, 1997: 27)

The theory that helps to explain Shuinear, and which forms part of
the theoretical framework for this thesis, is Bauman's (1989) ideas on
proximity. Gypsies and Travellers must be seen to be different, and
distant, from mainstream society so that they can take the burden of
faults and fears. Once they have taken this burden they can be
treated differently in discourse, and they can be controlled.

Berger and Luckmann's (1966) theory would suggest that the
distanced Gypsies and Travellers become a new objective reality,
and that the ensuing 'othering' discourse then becomes embedded
in an objective reality. The objective and subjective realities are self-
defining in a circular notion of discursive power. Elster's (1989)
explanation of social norms and Cohen's (1980) theory of folk devils
and moral panics frame the method by which groups can be othered
— through social norms. Gypsies and Travellers can be shown to
dispense with the societal norm of living in a settled house, society
then needs to 'other' them as a function to show people how not to
live. Various negative, subjective discourse is used to further distance
Gypsies and Travellers and this then becomes a new 'objective'
reality.

A range of theories, which explain society, norms and 'otherness'
support the links that Foucault (1977) makes between discourse and
control. They also suggest a motive behind the need to 'other'
Gypsies and Travellers. Firstly, by distancing Gypsies and Travel-

lers from the norm, it is easier on the collective conscience when they are treated badly. Secondly, the distanced group serve as a dumping ground for society's fears and faults.

Chapter Eight

Discursive Tools

Legislation, Policy and Practice

Introduction

> … discourse analysis emphasises the construction of social iden-
> tity in and through hegemonic practices of articulation, which
> partially fixes the meaning of social identities by inscribing them
> in the differential system of a certain discourse. (Torfing, 1999:
> 41)

The main focus of this chapter is that there are many and various
ways that Gypsies and Travellers are controlled in, and by, society.
It is a collection of tools, such as legislation and policy/practice,
inextricably linked within a discourse, which enforces control on
Gypsies and Travellers. One example, of the links between the discursive measures and physical control, is highlighted by Foucault
(1984b) in the development of state health programmes to control
the spread of disease. The culmination of policies resulted in the
physical structures of hospitals, but there was an emphasis on families taking control of the health of their own families. The scare of
disease and contagion still plays a part in moral panics today and
there is a perception that Gypsies and Travellers are 'dirty'. Morris
and Clements (2001) look at health initiatives targeted at Gypsies
and Travellers and it is possible to link state health policies with the
discussion on the control of Gypsies and Travellers. Foucault
(1984b) demonstrates discursive control translating into action, in
this instance the physical entity of hospitals. This translation of discourse into action is further exemplified in the examination of legislation and policy and practice.

There is a variety of ways in which Gypsies and Travellers are
controlled. The motive for the control measures is the perception

that Gypsies and Travellers are 'other', they are folk devils, not like 'us', and therefore they need to be controlled. This chapter aims to further demonstrate that language is not benign, but can be translated into controlling action. The two discursive tools analysed here are legislation, and policy and practice.

Legislation

Legislation is an overt tool to control all groups in society. Laws must be abided, or the consequence—if caught—is to pay a fine, provide a service to the community, or the ultimate sanction is to spend time in prison. As such, everyone is subject to legislation as a control mechanism. However, it would seem that Gypsies and Travellers are subject to tighter and less fair legislative control than members of the settled community.

Sandland (1996) in his paper *The Real, the Simulacrum, and the Construction of 'Gypsy' in Law* examines this notion; he describes his research as:

> ... a study of law as fantasy, as the constitution of marginality within yet outside marginality, and as the generation and reinvention of identity/difference. My topic is law's role in demarcating that double boundary which, first, separates travellers from the sedentary population and, secondly, sub-categorizes travellers into, on the one hand, 'real' or 'genuine' and on the other, the 'pretended' or 'simulated'. (Sandland, 1996: 383)

He goes on to examine the courts' interpretations of the Gypsy in law. On examining one particular case, he says:

> For the court in *Mills*, then, the essence of being a gypsy was the pursuit of a nomadic lifestyle and the absence of a fixed abode; a matter not of being, as Diplock LJ seemed to suggest, but of doing. (Sandland, 1996: 388)

The Criminal Justice and Public Order Act (1994) and Circular 1/94 was introduced to the Commons as a way of putting Gypsies and Travellers on an equal footing with regard to planning and self-help. The abolition of the duty to provide sites was excluded entirely from the political discourse in the House of Lords; and down-played in the Commons. Bancroft (2000) says as much:

> Of course, the forces that shape law-making and implementation are seldom if ever value free, substantively rational or disinterested. In addition to the broad social power relations which structure law-making and implementation, there are aspects of political expediency, horse-trading, outflanking or smoking out

of political rivals, all of which may be reflected in some way in the final legal text. Most of these processes can be identified in the production of the 1994 Act.

The Conservative government represented the parts of the 1994 Act affecting the planning regime as producing a planning system that was fairer all round.

(Bancroft, 2000: 48)

Planning legislation can be seen to play a large part in the control placed upon the nomadic lifestyle of Gypsies and Travellers. Different interpretations of the law mean that Gypsies and Travellers are even more disadvantaged as there is little clarity. The drafting and presentation of the Criminal Justice and Public Order Act (1994), and Circular 1/94, can be explained within my theoretical framework of discourse as control. The introduction of legislation in the Commons is the first phase of a circuitous route of interpretation of discourse, definition and redefinition. Once the wording of the law is agreed, it is then re-interpreted at the implementation stage. The hierarchy of the legislative system is theoretically separated into different powers so that those who create the law do not also implement it. However, the government can increasingly be seen to be involved in interpretation and implementation. Indeed, legislation introduced post 9/11 obfuscates the law even further and there is little transparency and openness. This is relevant here, because according to the framework, the question of who the control is for should ideally be 'society' as a whole; and who is doing the controlling should be the legislative. However, the hand of government can be seen in the interpretation of legislation and it is also proposed that it benefits government in that it can highlight society's fears (particularly post 9/11) and can then divert people from law which contravenes human rights and which allows for increased governmental control and policy shifts. My theoretical framework is useful, not just in looking at law and policy as it applies to Gypsies and Travellers, but in examining how the law is made and implemented in England.

Allen (2000) discusses the implementation of planning legislation at a local level:

Final decisions are made by council committees, consisting of councillors who are dependent for their position on election by voters. Politics, therefore, plays a large part in the decisions as do also personal prejudices of individual members of planning committees. Planning officials who deal with the applications in the first place, and make recommendations to the committees who decide on them, also have their prejudices, which are not as a rule, in favour of Gypsies. (Allen, 2000: 118)

This politicisation of planning decisions is echoed by Home (1994):

When gypsies move onto land without planning permission, or when councils propose sites for them, a hostile public reaction is virtually guaranteed. There will be front page coverage in the local, if not the national, press, and a flood of NIMBY (not in my back yard) objections. (Home, 1994: 111)

The Criminal Justice and Public Order Act (1994), together with Circular 1/94, is open to different interpretations across the country. The different interpretations of Circular 1/94 are demonstrated in the varying case law. The cases of Berry and Cooper were discussed in chapter two as exemplifying differing interpretations of the legal definition of a Gypsy in planning law. The definition and redefinition of Gypsy/Traveller in law is achieved through the circulatory framework. The motive for definition, even legal definition, can be seen to be politicised. The functionalist need to 'other' in legal cases is even more important as it sets precedents and provides a moral and legal code that people should adhere to. This also links to the question of how control is exercised, according to the framework. The use of legal discourse, and in particular legal definitions of Gypsy/Travellers (as opposed to self-definition as proposed by the travelling population and endorsed by the ODPM select committee in its report of 8th November 2004), serve to control through their interpretation. For instance Berry was interpreted (through legal discourse) to not be a Gypsy and therefore to be unsuccessful in his application for planning; yet Cooper was perceived to be a Gypsy at the stage of legal appeal. The legal definitions do not just stand alone as benign words; the discourse creates an opportunity to control.

The Homelessness Act (2002) is a further piece of legislation which can be examined here. Gypsies and Travellers should be included in local needs analyses under this piece of legislation, but Lord Avebury found that few local authorities were doing this on a practical level. The refusal of local authorities to analyse Gypsy/Traveller needs, under their legal duties, means that they are left out of strategic planning, and housing support is not being given as it should be. Refusal to implement is the translation tool from discourse into (non) action. Again, the motive is to distance Gypsy/Travellers from the mainstream settled population. However, in this case, rather than a general need to 'other', the motive may be linked to cost. If local authorities found out the needs of Gypsies and Travellers then they may have to meet them, and this would affect budgets. It would seem from Avebury's research that Gypsies and Travellers are being failed, on a strategic level, by local authorities who are not fulfilling their duties to consider their needs under the Homelessness Act 2002 (and more recently under the Housing Act, 2004). However, it is not just on a strategic basis that Gypsies and Travellers can be controlled under this legislation. On a practical level, Gypsies and Travellers who present as homeless are often forced to take bricks and mortar housing, in the absence of suitable Traveller accommodation. Crawley says this:

> ... reflects an implicit assumption that those in Travelling communities will eventually choose to move into permanent 'bricks and mortar' housing and will no longer travel ... many families do move into housing, sometimes willingly, sometimes not. (Crawley, 2004: 7)

Assimilation is a method of controlling and containing 'otherness'. Forcing Gypsies and Travellers to move into bricks and mortar housing, because of the lack of an alternative, is a strategic effort to achieve this level of control.

Hawes and Perez (1996) sum up the situation between the state and the Gypsy/Traveller, they too note the element of coercion:

> Even when, in 1968, the state acknowledged the legitimacy of a way of life quite alien to the notions of the house-dwelling majority and began to provide sites, still the law included unique prejudicial sanctions which were aimed at those very elements of travelling life which make it different from any other.
>
> In the words of one Traveller, it is as if the Gorgio is saying: 'Of course we must cater for your interesting differences, but we must encourage you, to the point of coercion, to stop being different — or at least make it as difficult as possible' (Hawes, 1994).
>
> (Hawes, 1996: 156)

However, there has been case-law which examined the offer of bricks and mortar housing to a homeless Gypsy family. The family turned down the offer because they said it was not suitable. The local authority felt that in making the offer of accommodation it had discharged its homelessness duty. The case was *R (on the application of Thomas Clarke) v Secretary of State for Transport Local Government and the Regions and Tunbridge Wells Borough Council (2002) EWCA Civ 819B*. The judge in the case said that where the applicant could prove that they had adhered to a travelling lifestyle and they had antipathy towards a house then 'the offer of bricks and mortar was as unsuit-

able as an offer of a rat infested barn'. This case was a triumph for
Gypsies and Travellers who felt that their different accommodation
needs were finally recognised, rather than covered up. However,
there was also the issue of 'proof' of adherence to a travelling lifestyle. This part of the judgement seems to be an attempt to distinguish between the 'real' and the 'simulacrum'. A more recent case,
however, did not follow this precedent. In Codona v Mid Bedfordshire District Council (as reported in The Times newspaper on 21st
July 2004) the offer of temporary Bed and Breakfast accommodation,
to Leanne Codona, was seen as a discharge of legal duties under the
Act, despite her aversion to bricks and mortar. So, the legal picture is
still unclear on where Gypsies and Travellers stand with regard to
offers of accommodation made under the homelessness legislation.

The conditions of the (failed) Traveller Law Reform Bill (2002)
demonstrated a balance of rights and responsibilities that seemed to
lean more heavily towards responsibilities for Gypsies and Travellers, than rights. It is often the case with Gypsies and Travellers that
the duties are much more onerous than the rights, which is reflected
in the Bill. The caveat on interference with the rights of Travellers is
quite wide in Section 8 of the Bill; it seems that it could be interpreted
quite widely in order to substantiate a claim for the need to interfere
with Travellers' rights. Additionally Schedule 2 is prescriptive:

SCHEDULE 2

HEALTH, SAFETY AND COMMUNITY CODE FOR GYPSIES AND TRAVELLERS

Keep groups small and inconspicuous. Anything more than six
vehicles is likely to be a problem but this will depend on the site
and proximity to other properties.

Consider your own health and safety. Space yourselves out and
keep the area clean and tidy.

Consider the dangers of fire, electric cables and generators and
passing traffic.

Look after the land you are on and consider nearby residents.

Do not dump or burn rubbish and leave the land clean and tidy.

Keep animals, especially dogs, under control ...

(Traveller Law Reform Bill, 2002: Schedule 2: 12)

The Traveller Law Reform Bill (2002) was viewed by many as a
progressive piece of proposed legislation, partly because of the duty
on local authorities to provide sites. This duty is important and it

was right that the Bill should be seen as a success in this regard. However, the onerous duties in the Schedule, rather than rights, seemed to be endorsing the link between Gypsies and anti-social behaviour. It is also interesting to examine who endorsed the Bill. The second signatory is Conservative MP Andrew MacKay. He referred to Gypsies and Travellers as 'scum' in his address to the House of Commons in January 2002 and yet he signed this Bill in July 2002 (perhaps to make amends?). If the Bill was a radical departure giving Gypsies and Travellers new rights to a nomadic lifestyle, whilst giving local authorities duties to provide sites, then an MP who thinks Gypsies are 'scum' would perhaps not have signed up to it.

Despite promises of new legislation to give Gypsies and Travellers the freedom to live their lives without undue interference, the law can be seen to control, rather than provide for. The law, divides Gypsies and Travellers between the 'real' and the 'fake' (Sandland, 1996), it controls the number of Travellers who can settle in one place and it is extremely prescriptive over the manner in which Gypsies and Travellers should conduct themselves. Whilst there has been case-law which identifies the difference between bricks and mortar offers and appropriate offers of accommodation for homeless families, there is still a practice of offering Gypsies and Travellers houses; and recent cases, such as the case Codona 2004, confirm this approach.

Legislative discourse, and its interpretation by the courts, is seen to be a tool of control within the theoretical framework, outlined previously. It is possible to see how the legal discourse can control Gypsies and Travellers, particularly through its use of legal definition, which denies some the label of Gypsy, and thereby finds against them in planning decisions. The question of why this particular tool is used, again, links back to the need to 'other' the group. It justifies the number of planning refusals for Gypsies and Travellers, compared with those for the settled population (see Bowers, 2004).

It is now necessary to take a brief look at the variety of ways in which the law is interpreted across different authority boundaries. The Criminal Justice and Public Order Act (1994) is used as an example to demonstrate the different ways in which the primary legislation is implemented within the context of local policies, practices and discourses.

Policy and Practice

The policy-implementation gap has been discussed already, particularly in the discussion on legislative control and how Section 61 of the Public Order Act (1994) is interpreted differently by varying police authorities. Policy is discussed further here in order to see how local authorities work within legislative constraints and how they interpret their duties to Gypsies and Travellers. In some instances policies are behind the mistrust between agencies and Gypsies and Travellers. In her work looking at the implementation of social services policy with regard to Gypsies and Travellers, Cemlyn (2000) says that:

> Social Services have become increasingly subject to the broader political context in their relationships with Travellers. However, there is also a specific history of troubled relationships. Welfare services in general, and in particular the threat to remove children from families, or their actual (and sometimes systematic) removal, have formed part of Travellers' historical experience of a state in Britain and elsewhere in Europe which was inimical to their way of life … (Cemlyn, 2000: 328)

As part of her research Cemlyn conducted a survey with all social services departments. She found that the Criminal Justice and Public Order Act (1994) had a low profile within social services because there was little engagement with Gypsies and Travellers. However, in comparison to other Gypsy/Traveller specific policy areas, it was near the top of the agenda. Nevertheless, there was a disparity with regard to the policies and actual implementation of the Act.

> In the first sample seven respondents (29.6%) replied that their authorities had engaged with policy around the CJPOA, and were among those respondents who indicated higher levels of engagement with Traveller issues generally. Reported attitudes varied widely, from a decision not to use the CJPOA, to taking a 'firm line' in relation to unauthorized camping. In a question related to interdepartmental coordination, inter-agency groups were the most frequently reported liaison mechanism (eight responses, 23.5%), and in five of these (14.7%) the focus of the groups was on the implications of the CJPOA. (Cemlyn, 2000: 331)

The different policy stances between local authorities, has also been in evidence during the literature review and data collection for this research. For instance, discussions took place with a number of Gypsy Traveller Liaison Officers and Planning Officers in different local authorities. In one area, although the duty to provide sites was repealed in 1994, the authority is using its discretionary power to examine the development of a new site; as part of its policy on meeting the needs of Gypsies and Travellers. Another local authority, more recently, is following the same route and is conducting a needs study. However, on the other hand, only two local authorities in the country successfully applied for ODPM funding for an emergency stopping site in 2003. A further council employed a Gypsy Liaison Officer who is well known amongst other professionals and who is an expert in the field; but she has been unable to facilitate any further site provision. The Criminal Justice and Public Order Act (1994) was followed to the letter in regard to new site provision in this area.

The mixed picture on site provision is indicative of differing interpretations of legislation and differing policies to deal with Gypsies and Travellers. The lack of consistency amongst local authorities makes it difficult for the travelling community to know where they stand. Their nomadic lifestyle means that they cannot become fully aware of their rights; instead they do not know how they will be treated from one district to the next. Indeed some local authorities purposefully do not include the development of new sites in their policy making, in case it attracts Travellers to the area. They feel that by not having a policy, Gypsies and Travellers will not come to their district. Some local authorities that are next door to an area with an adequate number of sites feel that the generous provision attracts more Gypsies and Travellers to the area and that they may cross local authority boundaries and set up unauthorised encampments. This mixed response to Gypsy/Traveller policy making does constrain the travelling lifestyle, and in some cases this is executed by negative proactivity. If there was a more uniform approach to implementing legislation, the situation would be clearer to both the travelling and settled communities. Instead obfuscation takes the place of possible clarity, and the lack of information can translate to a lack of power for Gypsies and Travellers. It is interesting to note the proactive use of 'textual silence' (Huckin, 2002) in some areas where the policy of site provision appears to be to not have a policy. Additionally, the varying interpretation of legislation makes for a confusing policy discourse; this lack of clarity also serves to control the travelling lifestyle of Gypsies as authorities can hide behind the ambiguity.

The differing interpretation of legislative powers and duties, by local authorities, is interesting. On a micro-level there is evidence of different motives at work (the why factor in the theoretical framework). For instance, the local authority that does not provide sites, or proactively seek to ascertain the needs of Gypsies and Travellers in their area may have two motives. Firstly, there is the issue of cost—

money needs to be found to build new sites. Linked to the issue of cost is the notion of politics and political power. As Marston (2002) discussed in his study, people want to distance themselves from groups perceived to be unpopular. Local councillors and MPs do not wish to align themselves with the needs of Gypsies and Travellers for fear of putting themselves at odds with the majority of voters and hence not being voted for at the next election.

Who is talking about Gypsies and Travellers?

This is an analytical theme from my primary research on the media. It is important to examine here because it has an effect on the mobilisation of discourse into action, for instance the implementation of legislation into policy and practice.

As part of the coding of the newspaper reports on Gypsies and Travellers, the origins of direct quotes were examined. Speech was put into 'ownership' nodes, for example: Travellers, local people, and politicians (councillors and Members of Parliament). The 'negative' comments in the articles were then analysed according to who had said them. Of the negative comments 26% were from political representatives of local constituencies — people who had been voted in by local members of the public to best represent their needs. Therefore, they could be seen to be speaking on behalf of local constituents.

It seems that the very people who should carefully consider what they say are the ones expounding negative images about Gypsies and Travellers. One such comment was analysed under the discursive theme of 'influx and invasion'; a Swindon Councillor said 'Hopefully, after all these years, we'll finally see an end to the illegal invasions which have caused so much misery and anger in this area' (*Western Daily Press*, 2003b: 25). In the same article, the South Swindon MP was quoted to be actively pursuing tougher laws to evict Travellers more efficiently.

Another Councillor in Grimsby talked about the costs associated with Travellers, and said '... increased costs of educating extra children and the potential tension caused by possibly hundreds of travellers moving into the area' (Turner, 2003: 10). The Chair of Stowe Town Council talked about abusive Gypsy youths and how female shopkeepers had to be protected from their intimidation during the Stowe fair (*Gloucestershire Echo*, 2003: 5). Two Birmingham Councillors showed their impatience in an article about moving Travellers on. They claimed that evictions were delayed because Traveller women claimed they were pregnant, and one of the Councillors referred to an example where a Traveller family was not moved on because one of their children was in hospital (Bell, 2003: 5).

Because of their status in the local community, what local Councillors and MPs say bears significance on the public discourse on Gypsies and Travellers. When elected officials use discriminatory language about Gypsies and Travellers it has the appearance of sanctioning the discriminatory discourse. This may be partly due to the fact that, as a group, Gypsies and Travellers are not vote winners and as such politicians are not interested in their needs. Crawley suggests as much: 'What was lacking was the political will to ensure that the accommodation needs of Travellers and Gypsies were addressed' (Crawley, 2004: 19).

Indeed, one could go further than a lack of political will. In some instances senior politicians have been as acquiescent as the public in allowing discriminatory discourse to unfairly label Gypsies and Travellers and mark them out for surveillance by society. In one extreme example of discriminatory discourse used in the House of Commons in 2002, the Conservative MP for Bracknell, Mr Andrew MacKay said:

> The cost to the college of further education, which is already hard pressed, is huge. The cost to council tax payers, where there are natural budgetary restraints, is great. Ordinary, innocent people – hard-working, normal, straightforward people who live around Bracknell – want to get on with their lives in peace, but they want protection under the law when they are invaded by this scum. They are scum, and I use the word advisedly. People who do what these people have done do not deserve the same human rights as my decent constituents going about their everyday lives. (MacKay, 2002)

This speech in the House of Commons was about a case where Travellers had set up an unauthorised encampment on a local college car park and the principal of the college felt that the police had taken too long to deal with the matter. MacKay's use of inflammatory and discriminatory language was not picked up by other members of parliament. Indeed, Angela Eagle (Under-secretary of State for the Home Office at the time) spoke of her gratitude to the Right Honourable Member for raising this. Eagle did state that Travellers should be seen as part of society, but she did not comment on the use of language by MacKay (Eagle, 2002). It could be suggested that, rather than just being acquiescent in a wider public discourse, politicians are motivated to 'other' particular groups in order to raise fear, so that political shifts are enabled (Cohen, 1980). Additionally, they may be motivated to keep costs of service provision down and there-fore want to use discourse to force Gypsies and Travellers to assimi-late into mainstream norms. This is where the political discourse affects the implementation of legislation and policy. Administrators may follow the discursive lead of politicians and will translate their duties or rights accordingly. This will not happen in all cases, which accounts for the different approaches to the treatment of Gypsies and Travellers in different local authority areas.

It should not be surprising therefore, that the language of local politicians and officials, as exemplified in the October 2003 news reports, is unfair towards Gypsies and Travellers. The example from the House of Commons is that it is acceptable to talk about Gypsies and Travellers in discriminatory language. This public discourse about Gypsies and Travellers contains so many socially constructed 'truths' that it does not seem to be noticed or commented upon. Unfortunately, this discourse does not seem to be improving its representations of Gypsies and Travellers. For instance, the Anti-social Behaviour Act (2003) contains new police powers to deal with Gypsies and Travellers under Part Seven. This sends out a distinct message that Gypsies and Travellers are anti-social; it further embeds the negative discourse surrounding Gypsies and Travellers.

Therefore, whilst at first the fact that 26% of the negative com-ments quoted in the October 2003 press were from local councillors and MPs may seem high, an examination of national political and public discourse goes some way to explaining this.

This chapter on legislation, policy and practice, and the impor-tance of who is talking about Gypsies and Travellers, has served to demonstrate the impact of discourse on the actions that affect the everyday lives of the travelling community. There is a problem of ambiguity in the interpretation of legislation which can be traced back to the different messages found in the national and local politi-cal discourse. Textual silence in local policy and the discourse of site provision indicates a level of control over Gypsies and Travellers. The words of the legislation are either adhered to rigidly (for instance there is no duty to provide sites) or they are ignored (but there is a power to provide sites). This equally applies to Section 61 of the 1994 Act where in some areas the police remove Gypsies and Travellers in a strict manner according to the letter of the law; or in other areas they suggest to local people that the law does not allow them to remove Gypsies and Travellers from unauthorised sites.

Local policy to interpret legislation, it would seem, is one of the tools that comprise the discourse used around Gypsies and Travellers.

Conclusion

This chapter has examined two main tools of control, within discourse: legislation, and policy and practice. Used together, these measures of control make the travelling lifestyle particularly difficult to maintain and it is suggested that assimilation with settled community 'norms' is the ultimate aim of such controlling measures. The reason for this aim may be linked to 'cost' of this alternative lifestyle.

The examination of who is talking about Gypsies and Travellers is important. If those with influence, local and national politicians, could understand more about the Gypsy/Traveller community then their discourse may change. If their discourse became less negative there may be an increased incentive for administrators to provide help to Gypsies and Travellers to the fullest of their legal capacity. The changed discourse in the political arena may, in an ideal world, influence the discourse of the media and the general public and there could be a positive move forward, as there has been in the case of other Black and Minority Ethnic groups. However, throughout this book the motive for 'othering' Gypsies and Travellers has been so compelling that it is difficult to imagine the discourse around Gypsies and Travellers, and the resultant actions, improving in the near future. If, as Shuinear (1997) suggests, that Gypsies and Travellers take on the fears of the Gaujos, then if the negative discourse around the travelling community stopped, which group would then take on the fears and problems of the settled community?

Chapter Nine

Moving On

The Current Position

Gypsies and Travellers have faced discrimination, and harassment, for centuries. However, unlike with other Black and Minority Ethnic groups, the public and political discourse has not improved over time. This book has dug beneath the surface of the discourse and has examined taken-for-granted notions of power and control, in a bid to explain why Gypsies and Travellers are 'othered' in this way.

The theoretical framework has been a helpful tool to explain the circular route of power in this particular relationship between the press/public and politicians and Gypsies and Travellers. Rather than stating that the travelling community is a controlled group, it has examined in detail how this works (through discourse and surveillance techniques) and why (to other the group, to make them take on the fears of society, to mask the real shifts in political debate by the government). It has been my intention that the book has examined the causes of the problem, as opposed to discussing the symptoms (a fundamental shortage of appropriate accommodation) again.

Some key discursive themes have been drawn out in the process of writing the book, these are outlined at figure two (chapter one) but they include issues around mess and cost, and they examine labelling and links to the folk devil. These themes resonate with other research in the field, but they are discussed within a theoretical frame of reference which helps us to understand why the control occurs.

So, how can the messages from this book help to improve the situation? On a practical level, I am not sure they can. Practical advice on increasing the amount of Gypsy/Traveller accommodation can be found in such research as Niner (2003) and Crawley (2004), but again they are looking at symptoms of the problem, not causes. If we are to really address the adverse discourse surrounding Gypsies and Travellers, and to temper this and therefore its end result which is the control of the group, then we need to look at the fundamental issues of the control and 'othering' of excluded groups.

Is There Motivation to Move On?

Shuinear (1997) said that we need a group on whom we can burden our fears. I take a similarly functionalist perspective to the problem. Society needs its demons, its others, to make the rest look as though it is working well. Rather than accepting that there are differences between people, the government wants those who don't fit in with a majority homogenous block, to be seen to be so different that they are not 'our' problem. Their difference is not celebrated; it is the cause of their (and 'our') problems. By making them different and distant they are blamed for stealing pets, murdering people, invading unauthorised sites, flouting the laws, evading taxes. The social construction of the Gypsy creates a demon on whom society can pin any problem, so as to distract attention from other issues. The motive for blaming Gypsies and Travellers for all of 'our' problems varies. The government can benefit by reducing expenditure on them, 'it is their fault we don't need to help them'. They can also benefit from raising the climate of fear about 'difference' in order to shield their policy shifts and power struggles. The media also benefits from reinforcing old stereotypes as they sell more newspapers, and make more money.

This is a depressing picture as it is difficult to see a way forward. Fundamentally, we need to reduce the distance between the settled community and Gypsies and Travellers; we need to understand more about each other. However, to do this requires real commitment from the government and from policy makers and it is not in their interest to help improve the situation.

There are moves, at government level, to address the issue of future site provision; however they will not go so far as to impose a legislative duty on local authorities. The Housing Act (2004) and the Homelessness Act (2002) require Gypsies and Travellers to be included in analyses of need. Additionally, the ODPM consultation and Circular 1/2006 examined the problems around the definition of Gypsies and Travellers. But, who is this for? Gypsies and Travellers must be fed up of the definition debate, they know who they are and would just like to be able to get on with their lives without harassment. The definition debate seems to be for the professionals and fundamentally, it will be non-Gypsies who define what a Gypsy is. The social construction of Gypsy finds its way into legislative and political debate again.

As mooted, the key for improving the current situation is to promote better understanding. But, do we want to? We need to put society's fears and blame onto someone, but if not Gypsies and Travellers, then who would take on this function? Let us look at who will benefit from promoting a better understanding between Gypsies and Travellers.

- Government? The government benefits from having Gypsies and Travellers as 'other' in order to pin blame for a variety of problems. Additionally they also add to the pattern of 'fear' which is heightened by politicians, in order that this will allow for political shifts and power games, without objections from the public. A scared society is easier to control and lead.

- Settled community? The settled community also benefits from 'othering' Gypsies and Travellers. As noted by Shuinear (1997) and Cohen (1980) the folk-devil takes on society's ills and it makes the majority feel better about themselves if their problems and faults are pinned onto a small minority who are made to be different.

- Media? The media benefit from folk-devils such as Gypsies and Travellers because, fundamentally, they sell newspapers and that means more money.

- Gypsies and Travellers? Yes, the travelling community would benefit from a better understanding between them and the settled community as they would face less harassment and perhaps also benefit from an increased provision of new sites and an inclusion in mainstream welfare policies such as health, education and housing.

If the main beneficiaries of an improved understanding between communities are Gypsies and Travellers, then there is little to drive the process forward. Government and the public seem not to care about the fate of Gypsies and Travellers. They assume they know who they are; indeed they define them in the media and in law for their own ends.

Next Steps

Gypsies and Travellers, and professionals who work with them, want to drive change forward. They want to see increased site provision, they want to monitor the media for discriminatory articles, and to prevent racial harassment. There are promising steps being taken, such as the Commission for Racial Equality's scrutiny project, the ODPM's guidance on needs assessment and Circular 1/2006 and the requirement to undertake accommodation needs analyses for Gypsies and Travellers (Housing Act 2004). However, these initiatives are addressing the symptoms again. Gypsies and Travellers need to be understood by the settled community and we need to be understood by them. This must be driven by government and the media; as we have seen in the discussion on who talks about Gypsies and Travellers, they have an enormous influence.

There is a hope that the situation for Gypsies and Travellers will improve and there are practical steps being taken to address this. I, however, have raised ideological problems which are far harder to tackle and which will take a long time to deal with.

Nevertheless, the practical initiatives which will follow in the coming years will start to move the ideological debate in the right direction. For instance, the new definitions in the replacement for Circular 1/94 may ease the problems in planning decisions for Gypsies and Travellers, so they can settle on their own land; where that is appropriate. It will be interesting to see whether all local authorities implement their duty under the Housing Act (2004) and undertake needs analyses for the travelling community, and outline potential sites in local development plans. Any incorporation of a Travellers' site in the local plan will kick-start public debate, and this point is crucial. If politicians and the media act responsibly and engage with positive discourse during the proceedings, then the public may follow and there may be a point when the folk-devil myth starts to be dispelled. As Duncan (1996) found, the reality of the Gypsy/Traveller was much more acceptable to the settled community, than the myth.

Central government, professionals who work with the travelling community, and groups such as the Gypsy Traveller Media Advisory Group (GTMAG) and the Gypsy Traveller Law Reform Coalition (GTLRC), all have their role to play in trying to change perceptions. If a practical, piecemeal approach is taken to shifting attitudes, then the situation may improve. The question has to be asked though; do enough people want to improve the situation for Gypsies and Travellers to allow for a fundamental shift in the pattern of discourse and control?

Bibliography

Acton, T (1974) *Gypsy Politics and Social Change*, London: Routledge and Kegan Paul

Acton, T (1994) "Modernisation, moral panics and the Gypsies" *Sociology Review*, September

Acton, T (Ed.) (1997) *Gypsy politics and Traveller identity*, Hertfordshire: University of Hertfordshire Press

Acton, T (2000) (Ed) *Scholarship and the Gypsy Struggle: Commitment in Romani Studies*, Hertfordshire: University of Hertfordshire Press

Acton, T and Mundy, G (Eds.) (1997) *Romani culture and Gypsy identity*, Hertfordshire: University of Hertfordshire Press

Akerstrom Anderson, N (2003) *Discursive Analytical Strategies, Understanding Foucault, Koselleck, Lacalau and Luhmann*, Bristol: The Policy Press.

Allen, D (2000) Gypsies and Planning Policy, in Acton, T (2000) *Scholarship and the Gypsy Struggle, Commitment in Romani Studies*, Hatfield: University of Hertfordshire Press

Anti-Social Behaviour Act 2003, London, HMSO, accessed through www.hmso.gov.uk/acts/acts2003/30038 – h.htm on April 24th 2004

Asthana, A (2004) Gypsies are new race hate target, *The Observer*, November 15th 2004, pg 5

Atkinson, R (1999) Discourses of Partnership and Empowerment in Contemporary British Urban Regeneration, *Urban Studies*, Vol. 36, No. 1, Pgs 59-72

Avebury, E (2004) Speech at the Traveller Law Reform Coalition, May 7th 2004: Birmingham

Bachrach, P & Baratz, M.S (1970) *Power and Poverty, theory and practice*, New York: Oxford University Press

Baird, R (2004) Economic Disaster Looms as 40,000 Head for Britain; Secret Plans to Halt the Gipsies, *The Express*, 22nd January 2004, Pg 8

Bancroft, A (2000) 'No Interest in Land': Legal and Spatial Enclosure of Gypsy-Travellers in Britain, *Space and Polity*, Vol. 4, No. 1, Pgs 41-56

Barkham, P (2004) Gypsies worker, 80, to return MBE in anger at policy, *The Guardian*, 10th August, Pg 5

Barnes, M, Sullivan, H and Matka, E (2003) *The Development of Collaborative Capacity in Health Action Zones, A Final Report from the National Evaluation*, Birmingham: University of Birmingham

Barthes, R (1977) "Inaugural Lecture, College de France", in Sontag, S (Ed) (1982) *Barthes, Selected Writings*, Oxford: The University Press

Basildon District Council v The First Secretary of State and Rachel Cooper (2003) EWHC 2621

Bauman, Z (1989) *Modernity and the Holocaust*, Oxford: Polity Press

BBC Radio Four (2004) *The Message*, February 6th

Becker, H.S (Ed.) (1964) *Perspectives on Deviance, The Other Side*, New York: The Free Press – a division of Macmillan Publishing Co

Bell, D (2003) Gypsy Curse, *Birmingham Evening Mail*, Midland Independent Newspapers plc, October 24th, Pg 5

Berger, P and Luckmann, T (1966) *The Social Construction of Reality, A Treatise in the Sociology of Knowledge*, Harmondsworth: Penguin Books Ltd

Beunderman, M (2004) *Roma MEP urges Commission to act for her people*, www.romea.cz/english/index.php (accessed on 11/8/04)

Bevir, M and Rhodes, R (2002) Interpretive Theory, in Marsh, D and Stoker, G (2002) (Eds) *Theory and Methods in Political Science*, (Second edition), Basingstoke: Palgrave Macmillan

Billig, M & Schegloff, E.A (1999) Critical Discourse Analysis and Conversation Analysis: and exchange between Michael Billig and Emanuel A. Schegloff, *Discourse and Society*, Vol. 10, No. 4, Pgs 543-582

Birmingham Evening Mail (2003) Brum is Gypsy Capital, *Birmingham Evening Mail*, Midland Independent Newspapers plc, October 24th, Pg 5

Blunkett, D (2002) Integration with Diversity: Globalisation and the Renewal of Democracy and Civil Society in Griffith, P and Leonard, M (Eds) (2002) *Reclaiming Britishness, Living Together after 11 September and the rise of the Right*. London: The Foreign Policy Centre

Bowers, J (2004) Against all odds, *Travellers Times*, Issue 19, Spring 2004

Bowers, J and Benjamin, A (2004) Pitch Battles, *The Guardian Society*, July 28th, Pg 2-3

Brayshay, C (2003) Stand by Tradition of See Fair Die, *The Northern Echo*, Newsquest North East Ltd, October 20th, Pg 23

Bristol Evening Post (2003) Travellers are flouting the law, *Bristol Evening Post*, Bristol United Press, October 7th, Pg 10

Brockes, E (2001) Wish you were here, *The Guardian*, www.guardian.co.uk/Refugees_in_Britain/Story May 21st, 2001

Cameron, D. Frazer, E. Harvey, P. Rampton, B. and Richardson, K (1999) Power/Knowledge: The Politics of Social Science, in Jarworski, A and Coupland, N (Eds.) (1999) *The Discourse Reader*, London: Routledge

Cemlyn, S (2000) Assimilation, control, mediation or advocacy? Social work dilemmas in providing anti-oppressive services for Traveller children and families, *Child and Family Social Work*, 2000, 5, Pgs 327-341

Channel 4 (2000) *Gypsies, Tramps and Thieves?* Documentary shown on January 29th

Clapham, D (1997) The Social Construction of Housing Management Research, *Urban Studies*, Vol. 34, Nos. 5-6, Pgs 761-774

Clapham, D (2002) Housing Pathways: A Post Modern Analytical Framework, *Housing Theory and Society*, Vol. 19, No.2, Pgs 57-68

Clark, C and Campbell, E (2000) 'Gypsy Invasion': A critical analysis of newspaper reaction to Czech and Slovak Romani asylum seekers in Britain, 1997, *Romani Studies* 5, Vol. 10, No. 1, Pgs 23-47

Clegg, S (1989) *Frameworks of Power*, London: Sage

Cloke, P; Milbourne, P; Widdowfield, R (2002) *Rural Homelessness – Issues, experiences and policy responses*. Bristol: Policy Press

Codona v Mid-Bedfordshire DC (2004) EWCA Civ 925, 15 July 2004

Cohen, S (1980) *Folk Devils and Moral Panics, The Creation of the Mods and Rockers*, Oxford: Martin Robertson

Cohen, S (1985) *Visions of Social Control*, Oxford: Polity Press

Cohen, S and Young, J (1973) (Eds) *The Manufacture of News, social problems, deviance and the mass media*, London: Constable

Colchester Borough Council (2003) Agenda and Reports for Public Planning Meeting December 16th

Commission for Racial Equality (2000) *Guidance for journalists – Travellers, Gypsies and the media*, http://www.cre.gov.uk/media/guidetj.html accessed on November 6th 2002

Community Development Project Political Economy Collective (1979) *The State and the Local Economy*, London: CDPPEC in association with PDC

Connors v The United Kingdom (2004) (application no. 66746/01), *Press release by the Registrar of the European Court of Human Rights*, http://press.coe.int/cp/2004/267a(2004).htm (accessed on June 4th 2004)

Connacht Tribune (1967) *On the Roadside*, Editorial, September 29th in Helleiner, J & Szuchewycz, B (1997) Discourses of Exclusion: The Irish Press and the Travelling People, in Riggins, S.H (Ed) (1997) *The Language and Politics of Exclusion*, London: Sage

Coolen H, Kempen E, Ozaki R (2002) Experiences and Meanings of Dwellings, *Housing, Theory and Society*, Vol. 19, No. 2, Pgs 114-116

Crawley, H (2004) *Moving Forward, the provision of accommodation for Travellers and Gypsies*, London: Institute of Public Policy Research

CRE v Dutton (1989) 1 AllER 306

Criminal Justice and Public Order Act (1994) London: HMSO

Cripps, J (1977) Accommodation for Gypsies: A report on the workings of the Caravan Sites Act, 1968, London, HMSO, in Niner, P (2003) *Local Authority Gypsy/Traveller Sites in England*, London: ODPM

Danaher, G; Schirato, T and Webb, J (2000) *Understanding Foucault*, London: Sage

Dandeker, C (1990) *Surveillance, Power & Modernity*, London: Polity Press

Darcy, M (1999) The Discourse of 'Community' and the Reinvention of Social Housing Policy in Australia, *Urban Studies*, Vol 36, No. 1, Pgs 13-26

Dean, M (1999) *Governmentality: Power and Rule in Modern Society*, London: Sage

Denscombe, M (2002) DBA Research Methodology class note, Leicester: De Montfort University

Department for Education and Skills (2003) *Aiming High: Raising the Achievement of Gypsy Traveller Pupils*, London: DfES

Department for the Environment (1994) *Circular 1/94*, London: DoE

Department of Environment, Transport and the Regions (1998) *Managing Unauthorised Camping, A Good Practice Guide*, London: DETR

Dodd, P (2002) The Challenge for New Labour in Griffith, P and Leonard, M (Eds) (2002) *Reclaiming Britishness, Living Together after 11 September and the rise of the Right*. London: The Foreign Policy Centre

Donzelot, J (1979) *The Policing of Families, Welfare Versus the State*, London: Hutchinson & Co

Doughty, S (2003) Axed, Queen of Looney Lotto Grants, *The Daily Mail*, 10th October, Pg 15

Duncan, T (1996) *Neighbours' views of official sites for travelling people*, Glasgow: The Planning Exchange

Durkheim, E (1989) *Suicide: a study in sociology*, London: Routledge

Eagle, A (2002) *House of Commons Hansard Debates*, Part 5, 15th January 2002, published on their website http://www.publications.parliament.uk/cgi-bin/ukparl_hl accessed on June 16th 2003

Earle, F. Dearling, A. Whittle, H. Glasse, R and Gubby, *A Time to Travel? An introduction to Britain's newer Travellers*, Dorset: Enabler Publications

East Midlands Today (2003) BBC1, 8am local news bulletin, August 29th 2003

Eco, U (1986) *Travels in Hyper-Reality*, translated by William Weaver, London: Pan Books Ltd

Eldridge, J (Ed.) (1993) *Getting the Message, News, Truth and Power*, London: Routledge

Ellinor, R (2003) Caravan Burned in Village Bonfire, *The Guardian*, October 30th London, Guardian Newspapers Ltd, Pg 7

Elster, J (1989) *The Cement of Society, A Study of Social Order*, New York: University of Cambridge

Erjavec, K (2001) Media representation of the discrimination against the Roma in Eastern Europe: the case of Slovenia, *Discourse and Society*, Vol. 12, No. 6, Pgs 699-727

Essex County Council Learning Services (1999) *One in a Million, A story of hardship, endurance and triumph in a Traveller family*, Essex: Essex County Council Learning Services

Fairclough, N (1992) *Discourse and Social Change*, Cambridge: Polity Press

Fairclough, N (1995) *Critical Discourse Analysis, the critical study of language*, London: Longman

Fairclough, N (2001) *Language and Power (2nd Ed)*, Harlow: Pearson Education Ltd

Flint, J and Rowlands, R (2003) Commodification, normalisation and intervention: Cultural, social and symbolic capital in housing consumption and governance, *Journal of Housing and the Built Environment*, Vol. 18, No. 3 Pgs 213-232

Fopp, R (2002) Increasing the Potential for Gaze, Surveillance and Normalisation: the transformation of an Australian policy for people who are homeless, *Surveillance and Society*, Vol. 1, No. 1, Pgs 48-65

Foucault, M (1966) *The Order of Things*, London: Routledge

Foucault, M (1969) *The Birth of the Clinic: An Archaeology of Medical Perception*, translated by A.M Sheridan, London: Tavistock Publications

Foucault, M (1972) *The Archaeology of Knowledge*, London: Routledge

Foucault, M (1977) *Discipline and Punish, The Birth of the Prison*, London: Penguin Books Ltd

Foucault, M (1976) *The History of Sexuality: 1 The Will to Knowledge*, London: Penguin Books Ltd

Foucault, M (1980) *Power/ Knowledge* edited by Colin Gordon, Harlow: Pearson Education Ltd

Foucault, M (1984a) *The History of Sexuality: 3 The Care of the Self*, London: Penguin Books Ltd

Foucault, M (1984b) The Politics of Health in the Eighteenth Century, in Rabinow, P (Ed.) (1984) *The Foucault Reader, An Introduction to Foucault's Thought*, London: Penguin Books

Foucault, M (1994) *Power* The Essential Works 3 edited by James D. Faubion, London: Penguin Press

Foucault, M (1999) The Incitement to Discourse (source Michel Foucault, The History of Sexuality: An Introduction, Translated by Robert Huxley, London: Penguin, 1978) in Jarworski, A and Coupland, N (Eds.) (1999) *The Discourse Reader*, London: Routledge

Foucault, M (2003) *Abnormal, Lectures at the College de France 1974-1975*, London: Verso

Fowler, R (1991) *Language in the News, Discourse and Ideology in the Press*, London: Routledge

Frost, J (1999) *Out of Sight, Out of Mind*, MSc Dissertation, unpublished, Leicester: De Montfort University

Galtung, J and Ruge, M (1973) Structuring and selecting news, in Cohen, S and Young, J (1973) (Eds) *The Manufacture of News, social problems, deviance and the mass media*, London: Constable

Gandy, O (1993) *The Panoptic Sort, A Political Economy of Personal Information*, Oxford: Westview Press

Gardiner, J (2004) Corporation will pay RSLs to build and manage Gypsy sites, *Housing Today*, 30th July, Pg 9

Garland, D (1990) *Punishment and Modern Society, A Study in Social Theory*, Oxford: Clarendon Press

Garland, D (2001) *The Culture of Control – crime and social order in contemporary society*, Oxford: Oxford University Press

Gerrard, N (2002) The face of human evil, *The Observer*, November 17th, pg 14

Giddens, A (1984) *The Constitution of Society: outline of the theory of Structuration*, Cambridge: Polity Press

Glasgow Media Action Group (1976) (Members of the group: Beharrell, P. Davis, H. Eldridge, J. Hewitt, J. Oddie, J. Philo, G. Walton, P. and Winston, B.) *Bad News*, London: Routledge

Gloucestershire Echo (2003) Hotline will Curb Fair Problems, *Gloucestershire Echo*, October 18th, Pg 5

Gould, A (1988) *Conflict and Control in Welfare Policy, The Swedish Experience*, London: Longman

Gramsci, A (1971) *Selections from the Prison Notebooks* Edited and translated by Quintin Hoare and Geoffrey Nowell Smith, Trowbridge: Redwood Books

Greenhill, S (2004) March of the Gipsy camps, *Daily Mail*, November 15th, 2004, Pg 1

Griffith, P and Leonard, M (Eds) (2002) *Reclaiming Britishness, Living Together after 11 September and the rise of the Right*. London: The Foreign Policy Centre

Gurney, C (1990) *The Meaning of Home in the Decade of Owner Occupation, Towards and Experiential Research Agenda*, Working Paper 88, Bristol, School for Advanced Urban Studies, Bristol University

Gurney, C (1997) Pride and Prejudice: Discourses of Normalisation in Public and Private Accounts of Home Ownership, *Housing Studies*, Vol. 14, No. 2, 163-183

Gurney, C (1999) Lowering the Drawbridge: A Case Study of Analogy and Metaphor in the Social Construction of Home-ownership, *Urban Studies*, Vol. 36, No 10, Pgs 1705-1722

Gypsy & Traveller Media Advisory Group (2003) *Constitution*

Habermas, J (1987) *The Philosophical Discourse of Modernity: twelve lectures*, Cambridge: Polity Press

Hancock, I (2002) *We are the Romani People*, Hatfield: University of Hertfordshire Press

Harloe, M (1995) *The People's Home? Social Rented Housing in Europe and America*, Oxford: Blackwell

Hastings, A (1998) Connecting Linguistic Structures and Social Practices: a Discursive Approach to Social Policy Analysis, *Journal of Social Policy*, Vol, 27, No 2, Pgs 191-211

Hastings, A (1999a) Analysing Power Relationships in Partnerships: Is there a Role for Discourse Analysis? *Urban Studies*, Vol. 36, No. 1, Pgs 91-106

Hastings, A (1999b) Discourse and Urban Change: Introduction to the Special Issue, *Urban Studies*, Vol. 26, No. 1, Pgs 7-12

Hastings, A (2000) Discourse Analysis: What Does it Offer Housing Studies? *Housing Theory and Society* Vol. 17, No. 3 pages 131-139

Hawes, D and Perez, B (1996) *The Gypsy and the State* 2nd Ed. Bristol: The Policy Press

Haworth, A and Manzi, T (1999) Managing the 'Underclass': Interpreting the Moral Discourse of Housing Management, *Urban Studies*, Vol. 36, No.1, Pgs 153-165

Helleiner, J & Szuchewycz, B (1997) Discourses of Exclusion: The Irish Press and the Travelling People, in Riggins, S.H (Ed) (1997) *The Language and Politics of Exclusion*, London: Sage

Heuss, H (2000) Anti-Gypsyism Research: The Creation of a New Field of Study, in Acton, T (2000) *Scholarship and the Gypsy Struggle, Commitment in Romani Studies*, Hatfield: University of Hertfordshire Press

Hier, S (2003) Probing the Surveillant Assemblage: on the dialectics of surveillance practices as processes of social control, *Surveillance and Society*, Vol. 1, No. 3, Pgs 399-411

Hilditch, M (2005) ODPM takes Gypsies and Travellers' side in sites row, *Housing Today*, 11th March, Pg 9

Holloway, S (2002) Outsiders in rural society? Constructions of rurality and nature-social relations in the racialisation of English Gypsy-Travellers, 1869-1934, *Environment and Planning D: Society and Space*, Vol. 21, Pages 695-715

Home, R (1994) The planner and the gypsy, in Thomas, H and Krishnarayan, V (1994) (Eds) *Race Equality and Planning, Policies and Procedures*, Aldershot: Avebury

Housing Today (2004) Lib Dem peer says Gypsy sites must be run by local authorities, not RSLs, *Housing Today*, 15th October, 2004, Pg 12

Huckin, T (2002) Textual silence and the discourse of homelessness, *Discourse and Society*, Vol. 13, No. 3, Pgs 347-372

Hutton, Lord (2004) *Report of the Inquiry into the Circumstances Surrounding the Death of Dr David Kelly C.M.G*, London: House of Commons

Inside Housing (2004) *Court rules gypsies have same rights as tenants*, Inside Housing, June 4th, Pg 8

Jacobs, K (1999) Key Themes and Future Prospects: Conclusion to the Special Issue, *Urban Studies*, Vol. 36, No. 1, Pgs 203-213

Jacobs, K. Kemeny, J and Manzi, T (2003) Power, Discursive Space and Institutional Practices in the Construction of Housing Problems, *Housing Studies*, Vol. 18, No. 4, Pgs 429-446

Jacobs, K, Kemeny, J and Manzi, T (Eds) (2004) *Social Constructionist Methods in Housing*, Aldershot: Ashgate

Jarworski, A and Coupland, N (Eds.) (1999) *The Discourse Reader*, London: Routledge

Johnston, P (2002) Blunkett's warning to asylum seekers *The Daily Telegraph* September 21st, Pg 10

Johnston, P (2004) MPs in call for more official gipsy camps, *The Daily Telegraph*, November 8th, 2004, Pg 4.

Kellner, D (2003) *Media Spectacle*, New York: Routledge

Kelly, T (2004) £350,000 That's the bill (so far) to evict 450 travellers from their illegal camp, *Daily Mail*, 1st November 2004, Pg 31

Kemeny, J (1992) *Housing and Social Theory*, London: Routledge

Kemeny, J (2002) Reinventing the Wheel? The Interactional Basis for Social Constructionism, *Housing, Theory and Society*, Vol. 19, Nos 3-4, Pgs 140-141

Kennedy, R (2002) *Nigger, The Strange Career of a Troublesome Word*, New York: Pantheon Books

Kenrick, D (Ed.) (1999) *In the shadow of the Swastika, The Gypsies during the Second World War 2*, Hertfordshire: Centre de recherches tsiganes and University of Hertfordshire Press

Kenrick, D and Clark, C (1999) *Moving On, The Gypsies and Travellers of Britain*, Hatfield: University of Hertfordshire Press

King, P (2004) Relativism, subjectivity and the self: A critique of social constructionism, in Jacobs, K, Kemeny, J and Manzi, T (Eds) (2004) *Social Constructionist Methods in Housing*, Aldershot: Ashgate

Kundnani, A (2004) Express newspaper faces criticism from its own journalists for anti-Roma stance, Independent race and refugee news network, February 4th, 2004, http://www.irr.org.uk/2004/february/ak000006.html accessed on February 6th 2004

Leudar, I and Nekvapil, J (2000) Presentations of Romanies in the Czech media: on category work in television debates, *Discourse and Society*, Vol. 11, No. 4, Pgs 487-513

Levin. T, Frohne. U and Weibel. P (Eds) (2002) *CTRL SPACE, Rhetorics of Surveillance from Bentham to Big Brother*, London: The MIT Press

Levinson, M and Sparkes, A (2003) Gypsy Masculinities and the School-Home Interface: exploring contradictions and tensions, *British Journal of Sociology of Education*, Vol. 24, No. 5, Pgs 587-603

Levitas, R (1998) *The Inclusive Society: Social Exclusion and New Labour*, Basingstoke: Macmillan

Levy, A (2004) Village in dread of travellers who sent the builders in first, *Daily Mail*, Pg 27

Lianos, M (2003) Social Control after Foucault, *Surveillance and Society*, Vol. 1, No. 3, Pgs 412-430

Lincolnshire Free Press (2004) Travellers' site ruling 'invitation to anarchy', *Lincolnshire Free Press*, 5th October, 2004, Pg 3

Lipsky, M (1980) *Street-Level Bureaucracy, Dilemmas of the Individual in Public Services*, New York: Russell Sage Foundation

Lodge, A (2004) What Happened Next? *Observer Magazine*, March 28th, 2004, Pg 65

Lodge, A (undated) *All about my 'BIG BROTHER'*, http://tash.gn.apc.org/watched1.htm accessed on November 6th 2002

London Borough of Newham (2003) *Unauthorised Encampments and Associated Illegal Activity*, Report to the Mayor

Long, R (2004) Travellers vow to fight to stay at site, *Lincolnshire Free Press*, September 14th, 2004, Pg 5

Lowndes, V (2001) Rescuing Aunt Sally: Taking Institutional Theory Seriously in Urban Politics, *Urban Studies*, Vol. 238, No. 11, Pgs 1953-1971

Lukes, S (1974) *Power: A Radical View*, Basingstoke: Macmillan Press Ltd

Lukes, S (Ed.) (1986) *Power* Oxford: Basil Blackwell Ltd

Lyon, D (2001) *Surveillance Society, Monitoring everyday life*, Buckingham: Open University Press

Lyon, D (2002) Editorial. Surveillance Studies: Understanding visibility, mobility and the phenetic fix, *Surveillance and Society*, Vol. 1, No. 1, Pgs 1-7

Lyon, D (Ed) (2003) *Surveillance As Social Sorting, Privacy, Risk and Digital Discrimination*, London: Routledge

Machiavelli, N (1961) *The Prince*, Translation by George Bull, Harmondsworth: Penguin

MacKay, A (2002) *House of Commons Hansard Debates*, Part 5, 15th January 2002, published on their website http://www.publications.parliament.uk/cgi-bin/ukparl_hl accessed on June 16th 2003

Marsh, D and Furlong, P (2002) A Skin, not a Sweater: Ontology and Epistemology in Political Science, in Marsh, D and Stoker, G (2002) (Eds) *Theory and Methods in Political Science*, (Second edition), Basingstoke: Palgrave Macmillan

Marsh, D and Stoker, G (2002) (Eds) *Theory and Methods in Political Science*, (Second edition), Basingstoke: Palgrave Macmillan

Marston, G (2000) Metaphor, morality and myth: a critical discourse analysis of public housing policy in Queensland, *Critical Social Policy*, Vol. 20, No. 3, Pgs 349-373

Marston, G (2002) Critical Discourse Analysis and Policy-Orientated Housing Research, *Housing Theory and Society*, Vol. 19, No. 2, Pgs 82-91

Marston, G (2004) Managerialism and Public Housing Reform, *Housing Studies*, Vol. 19, No. 1, Pgs 5-20

Marx, K (1999) *Capital* (A New Abridgement – edited and notes by David McLellan) New York: Oxford University Press

Mayall, D (1995) *English Gypsies and State Policies*, Hatfield: University of Hertfordshire Press

Mayall, D (2004) *Gypsy Identities 1500-2000, From Egipcyans and Moon-Men to the Ethnic Romany*, Routledge: London

McCready, T and J. (2001) *A Wandering of Gypsies*, Derbyshire: Robert Dawson

McCrystal, C (2000) Seeking a safe Haven, *Evening Standard*, 31st March, Pg 7

McLaughlin, D (2005) Gypsies fight for justice over forced sterilisation, *The Observer*, 22nd May, Pg 22

McNay, L (1994) *Foucault a critical introduction* Cambridge: Polity Press

Means, R (1977) *Social Work and the 'Undeserving' Poor* (Occasional Paper 37), Birmingham: Centre for Urban and Regional Studies, University of Birmingham

Meyer, M (2001) "Between theory, method, and politics: positioning of the approaches to CDA" in Wodak, R and Meyer, M (2001) *Methods of Critical Discourse Analysis*, London: Sage

Meyrowitz, J (1987) *No Sense of Place: The Impact of Electronic Media on Social Behaviour*, Oxford: Oxford University Press

Morley, D (2000) *Home Territories, Media, Mobility and Identity*, London: Routledge

Morris, J and Winn, M (1990) *Housing and Social Inequality*, London: Hilary Shipman

Morris, R (1998) Gypsies and the Planning System, *Journal of Planning and Environmental Law*, July, Pgs 635-643

Morris, R (1999) The Invisibility of Gypsies and Other Travellers, *The Journal of Social Welfare and Family Law*, Vol. 21, No. 4, Pgs 397-404

Morris, R (2000) Gypsies, Travellers and the Media: Press regulation and racism in the UK, *Communications Law*, Vol. 5, No. 6 Pgs 213-219

Morris, R (2001) Gypsies and Travellers: new policies, new approaches, *Police Research and Management*, Vol 5, No. 1, Pgs 41-49

Morris, R (2003) *Romaphobia: Animosity, Exclusion, Invisibility and Travelling People in the UK*, PhD Thesis, Cardiff: Cardiff University

Morris, R and Clements, L (Eds.) (1999) *Gaining ground: Law reform for Gypsies and Travellers*, Hatfield: University of Hertfordshire Press

Morris, R and Clements. L (2001) *Disability, Social Care, Health and Travelling People*, Cardiff: Cardiff Law School

Morris, R and Clements, L (2002) *At What Cost? The economics of Gypsy and Traveller encampments*, Bristol: Policy Press

Mumby, D (Ed.) (1993) *Narrative and Social Control: Critical Perspectives*, London: Sage

Murray, C (1990) *The Emerging British Underclass*, London: IEA Health and Welfare Unit

Murray, C (1994) *Underclass: The Crisis Deepens*, London: IEA Health and Welfare Unit

National Farmers' Union (2003) *Britain's Rural Outlaws*, www.nfu.co.uk accessed on 5th February 2004

Neuendorf, K.A (2002) *The Content Analysis Guidebook*, London: Sage

Niner, P (2002) *The Provision and Condition of Local Authority Gypsy/Traveller Sites in England*, London: ODPM

Niner, P (2003) *Local Authority Gypsy/Traveller Sites in England*, London: ODPM

Niner, P (2004a) Accommodating Nomadism? An Examination of Accommodation Options for Gypsies and Travellers in England, *Housing Studies*, Vol. 19, No. 2, Pgs 141-159

Niner, P (2004b) *Counting Gypsies and Travellers: A Review of the Gypsy Caravan County System*, London: ODPM

Nunan, D (1993) *Introducing Discourse Analysis*, London: Penguin Books Ltd

O'Flynn, P (2004) Daily Express Victory as Blair does U-Turn on Immigrants; Gypsies: You Can't Come In, *The Express*, 5th February, Pgs 1 & 2

Office of the Deputy Prime Minister (1994) *Circular 01/94: Gypsy Sites and Planning*, London: ODPM

Office of the Deputy Prime Minster Select Committee: Housing, Planning, Local Government and the Regions (2004), *Gypsy and Traveller Sites, Thirteenth Report of Session 2003-04*, London: House of Commons

Patrin (2000) *The Patrin Web Journal, Timeline of Romani (Gypsy) History)*, http://www.geocities.com/Paris/5121/timeline.htm accessed on March 23rd, 2004

Perlesz, A and Lindsay, J (2003) Methodological triangulation in researching families: making sense of dissonant data, *International Journal of Social Research Methodology*, Vol. 6, No. 1, Pgs 25-40

Philo, G (Ed.) (1999) *Message Received*, Essex: Addison Wesley Longman Ltd

Planning and Compulsory Purchase Act (2004) London: House of Commons

Planning Officer (2004) Colchester Borough Council, interview by telephone, February 10th

Power, A (1987) *Property Before People, The Management of Twentieth-century Council Housing*, London: Harper Collins

Prescott, 2002 The Heart and Soul of the Nation, *The Guardian*, January 16th, Pgs 4-5

R (on the application of Thomas Clarke) v Secretary of State for Transport Local Government and the Regions and Tunbridge Wells Borough Council (2002) EWCA Civ 819B

Rabinow, P (Ed.) (1984) *The Foucault Reader*, London: Penguin

Reisigl, M and Wodak, R (2001) *Discourse and Discrimination, Rhetorics of Racism and Anti Semitism*, London: Routledge

Riddell, M (2002) The monsters in our midst, *The Observer*, September 15th, Pg 22

Riggins, H (1997) The Rhetoric of Othering, in Riggins, H (1997) (Ed.) *The Language and Politics of Exclusion, Others in Discourse*, London: Sage

Riggins, S.H (Ed) (1997) *The Language and Politics of Exclusion*, London: Sage

Risman, B (2002) Tony Taking Action on Bogus Asylum Seekers, *The Law Journal*, www.thelawjournal.co.uk May 23rd, 2002

Room, G (1995) *Beyond the Threshold, the measurement and analysis of social exclusion*, Bristol: The Policy Press

Rose, N (1999) *Powers of Freedom: reframing political thought*, Cambridge: University Press

Rousseau, J-J (1994) a translation by Christopher Betts *The Social Contract*, Oxford: Oxford University Press

Sandland, R (1996) The Real, the Simulacrum, and the Construction of 'Gypsy' in Law, *Journal of Law and Society*, Vol. 23, No. 3, Pgs 383-405

Sardar, Z (2002) The Excluded Minority: British Muslim Identity After 11 September in Griffith, P and Leonard, M (Eds) (2002) *Reclaiming Britishness, Living Together after 11 September and the rise of the Right.* London: The Foreign Policy Centre

Saugeres, L (1999) The Social Construction of Housing Management Discourse: Objectivity, Rationality and Everyday Practice, *Housing, Theory and Society*, Vol. 16, No.2, Pgs 93-105

Saugeres, L and Clapham, D (1999) Themes and Contradictions in Housing Management: An Analysis of Bureaucratic Discourse, *Netherlands Journal of Housing and the Built Environment*, Vol. 13, No. 3, Pgs 257-276

Sawer, P (2000) Digging in Against Travellers, *Evening Standard*, 21st September, Pg 11

Schegloff, E.A (1987) Between Micro and Macro: Contexts and Other Connections, in Alexander, J et al (Eds) (1987) *The Micro-Macro Link*, London: University of California Press

Schegloff, E.A (1997) Whose text? Whose context? *Discourse and Society*, Vol. 8, No. 2, Pgs 165-187

Schegloff, E.A. Koshik I, Jacoby S and Olsher, D (2002) Conversation Analysis and Applied Linguistics, *Annual Review of Applied Linguistics*, 22, Pgs 3-31

Schoeman, F.D. (1992) *Privacy and Social Freedom*, Cambridge: Cambridge University Press

Scruton (2001) *The Meaning of Conservatism*, Basingstoke: Palgrave

Shuinear, S (1997) Why do Gaujos hate Gypsies so much, anyway? In Acton, T (Ed.) (1997) *Gypsy politics and Traveller identity*, Hertfordshire: University of Hertfordshire Press

Sibley, D (1995) *Geographies of exclusion: society and difference in the West*, London: Routledge

Smart, H. Titterton, M and Clark, C (2003) A literature review of the health of gypsy/traveller families in Scotland: the challenges for health promotion, *Health Education*, Vol. 103, No. 3, Pgs 156-165

Smith, M and Taffler, R.J (2000) The Chairman's Statement: A Content Analysis of Discretionary Narrative Disclosures, *Accounting, Auditing and Accountability*, Vol. 13, No. 5, Pgs 624-646

Smithson, J (2000) Using and analysing focus groups: limitations and possibilities, *International Journal of Social Research*, Vol. 3, No. 2, Pgs 103-119

Snow, E (2004) Nomad's Land, *Housing Today*, 3rd September 2004, Pg 21-24

Social Exclusion Unit (1998) *Bringing Britain together: a national strategy for neighbourhood renewal*, London: Cabinet Office

Social Exclusion Unit (2001) *A New Commitment to Neighbourhood Renewal, National Strategy Action Plan*, London: Cabinet Office

Social Exclusion Unit (2004) *Tackling Social Exclusion: Taking stock and looking to the future, emerging findings*, London: Office of the Deputy Prime Minister

South Wales Evening Post (2003) Stones Moved as Travellers Arrive, *South Wales Evening Post*, October 3rd, Pg 2

Staples, W (2000) *Everyday Surveillance, Vigilance and Visibility in Postmodern Life*, Oxford: Rowman & Littlefield Publishers Inc

Stenson, K and Watt, P (1999) Governmentality and 'the Death of the Social'?: A Discourse Analysis of Local Government Texts in South-east England, *Urban Studies*, Vol. 36, No. 1, Pgs 189-201

Stewart, M (1997) The puzzle of Roma persistence: group identity without a nation. In Acton, T and Mundy, G (Eds.) (1997) *Romani culture and Gypsy identity*, Hertfordshire: University of Hertfordshire Press

Steyn, M (1988) All Venusians now, sentimentality in the media. In Anderson, D and Mullen, P *Faking It, The Sentimentalisation of Modern Society*, London: Social Affairs Unit

Stroll, A (2002) *Wittgenstein*, Oxford: OneWorld

Stubbs, M (1996) *Text and Corpus Analysis, computer assisted studies of language and culture*, Oxford: Blackwell Publishers Ltd

Ten Have, P (1999) *Doing Conversation Analysis*, London: Sage

Thatcher, M (1993) *The Downing Street Years*, New York: Harper Collins

The Cornishman (2003a) I Don't Think So, *The Cornishman*, October 23rd, Pg 35

The Cornishman (2003b) Come and Meet Your Nomadic Neighbours, *The Cornishman*, October 23rd , Pg 35

The Guardian (2004) False Figures, *The Guardian*, 21st January 2004, Pg 25

The Housing Bill (2003) London: House of Commons

The Times (2004) Law Report (Codona v Mid Bedfordshire District Council), 21st July

This is Wiltshire (2003) £60,000 to keep them out, October 6th 2003, *This is Wiltshire*, Pg 1

This is Worcestershire (2003) £50,000 mess bill, *This is Worcestershire* October 27th, Pg 9

Thomas, H and Krishnarayan, V (1994) (Eds) *Race Equality and Planning, Policies and Procedures*, Aldershot: Avebury

Thomas, P and Campbell, S (1992) *Housing Gypsies*, Cardiff: Cardiff Law School

Thorpe, N (2002) Romania closes door on gypsies, *BBC News*, http://news.bbc.co.uk/2/hi/europe October 4th, 2002

Tong, D (1998) (Ed.) *Gypsies: an interdisciplinary reader*, Hatfield: University of Hertfordshire Press

Tong, D (1998) *Gypsies: An Interdisciplinary Reader*, London: Garland Science

Torfing, J (1999) *New Theories of Discourse: Laclau, Mouffe and Zizek*, Oxford: Blackwell

Traveller Law Reform Unit (2002) *Traveller Law Reform Bill*, London: House of Commons

Turner, L (2003) Benefit reforms to present problems, *Grimsby Evening Telegraph*, October 11th, Pg 10

Turner, R (2000) Gypsies and Politics in Britain, *The Political Quarterly*, Vol. 71, No. 1, Pgs 68-77

Turner, R (2002) Gypsies and British Parliamentary Language: An Analysis, *Romani Studies* 5, Vol. 12, No. 1, Pgs 1-34

Van Cleemput, P and Parry, G (2001) Health status of Gypsy Travellers, *Journal of Public Health Medicine*, Vol. 23, No. 2, Pgs 129-134

Van Dijk, T (1993) Stories and Racism, in Mumby, D (Ed.) (1993) *Narrative and Social Control: Critical Perspectives*, London: Sage

Van Dijk, T (1999a) On Context, *Discourse and Society*, Vol. 10, No. 3, Pgs 291-292

Van Dijk, T (1999b) Critical Discourse Analysis and Conversation Analysis, *Discourse and Society*, Vol. 10, No. 4, Pgs 459-460

Vaz, P and Bruno, F (2003) Types of Self-Surveillance: from abnormality to individuals 'at risk', *Surveillance and Society*, Vol. 1, No. 3, Pgs 272-291

Watt, N (2001) Hague pledges hard line on unwed mothers and travellers, *Guardian Society*, http://society.guardian.co.uk May 8th, 2001

Watt, P and Jacobs, K (2000) Discourses of Social Exclusion, *Housing Theory and Society*, Vol. 17, No. 1, Pgs 14-26

Weber, R.P (1990) *Basic Content Analysis (2nd Ed)* London: Sage

Webster, L and Millar, J (2001) *Making a living: Social security, social exclusion and New Travellers*, Bristol: The Policy Press

Weckmann, S (1998) Researching Finnish Gypsies: Advice from a Gypsy, in Tong, D (1998) (Ed.) *Gypsies: an interdisciplinary reader*, Hatfield: University of Hertfordshire Press

Western Daily Press (2003a) Gypsies face vicious prejudice, *Western Daily Press*, October 29th, Pg 6

Western Daily Press (2003b) The End of the Road for Travellers in Town, *Western Daily Press*, October 10th, Pg 25

Western Daily Press (2003c) Travellers are Not Gypsies, *Western Daily Press*, October 15th, Pg 12

Widdowson, H.G (1995) Discourse Analysis: a critical view, *Language and Literature*, Volume 4, Number 3, Pages 157-172, London: Sage

Wilkins, S (1973) Information and the definition of deviance, in Cohen, S and Young, J (1973) (Eds) *The Manufacture of News, social problems, deviance and the mass media*, London: Constable

Wilson, D (2002) Speaking in a debate on BBC Radio Four's *Today* programme, 25th October

Wittgenstein, L (1974) *Tractacus logico-philosophicus*, London: Routledge and Kegan Paul

Wodak, R and Meyer, M (2001) *Methods of Critical Discourse Analysis*, London: Sage

Wood, D (2003) Editorial. Foucault and Panopticism Revisited, *Surveillance and Society*, Vol. 1, No. 3, Pgs 234-239

Wrexham County Borough Council v National Assembly for Wales and Berry (2003) EWCA Civ 835

Wright, J (2003) Preparing for an influx of travellers, *Grimsby Evening Telegraph*, October 4th, Pg 8

Zelizer, B (1993) Narratives of Self-Legitimation, in Mumby, D (1993) (Ed) *Narrative and Social Control: Critical Perspectives*, London: Sage

Index